Also in the Crafts Series from Little, Brown
Gerald Clow, General Editor

BLACK AND WHITE PHOTOGRAPHY
Henry Horenstein

CROCHET
Mary Tibbals Ventre

POTTERY
Cora Pucci

LEATHERWORK
Benjamin Maleson

WOODWORKING
Raphael Teller

OFF-LOOM WEAVING
Elfleda Russell

STAINED GLASS
Barbara and Gerry Clow

NEEDLEPOINT
Carol Huebner Collins

Forthcoming

SUPER 8 PHOTOGRAPHY
Barry Schonhaut

Also by Nicholas Humez

The Boston Basin Bicycle Book
(with Alex Humez, Edward Goldfrank, and Janice Goldfrank)

Latina pro Populo
(with Alex Humez)

SILVERSMITHING

A Basic Manual

SILVERSMITHING

A Basic Manual

NICHOLAS D. HUMEZ

LITTLE, BROWN AND COMPANY—BOSTON—TORONTO

First Edition

T 05/76

Library of Congress Cataloging in Publication Data

Humez, Nicholas
  Silversmithing.

  (Little, Brown craft series)
  1. Silverwork—Amateurs' manuals.   I.   Title.
TS730.H85   739.2'3   76-1993
ISBN 0-316-38151-9

Published simultaneously in Canada
by Little, Brown & Company (Canada) Limited

Printed in the United States of America

To

David Ernest Humez, my father, who first showed me the use of tools;
Josephine Eckert Diggs, who first encouraged me to draw;
Faith Leah Dunne, who taught me to write freely;
and Sally Thorpe Smith, who called my attention to silver.

Fulgebunt quasi splendor firmamenti.
(West wall, Sanders Theater, Harvard University)

Acknowledgments

I am indebted to Peter Hunsberger, photographer for Cora Pucci's *Pottery* earlier in the Little, Brown Craft Series, for suggesting to the series editor that I be asked to write the present book; I am grateful to editors Richard McDonough and Deborah Salem for acting on that suggestion, for championing the cause of this book within the company, and for invaluable assistance in preparing a comprehensible manuscript for publication. Our task was made a great deal easier by Susan Middleton, who typed the fair copy of the manuscript from my intermediate draft, and by Michael Mattil, who copy edited the manuscript, both of whom caught and queried errors in syntax, punctuation, and usage which I had missed.

I have been actively helped by several of my fellow silversmiths, who have given generously of their time and expertise in reading parts of the manuscript for accuracy and clarity, supplied me with first-hand information about techniques with which they had more practical experience than I, and permitted me to photograph their work to illustrate my text. These include Tom Brown and Leslie Wind, of Rockport, Massachusetts; Douglas and Miriam French and Michael Moore, of Burlington, Vermont; Robin Wilmott and Michael Allen, of Cambridge, Massachusetts; Warren Lee, of Hartford, Connecticut, and Peter Indorf, of New Haven, Connecticut. For information about related fields I am grateful to Chris Murch, pewtersmith of Rockport, Massachusetts; Boston etcher and scrimshander Peter Wayne Blumberg; broadaxeman Ross Faneuf of Brentwood, New Hampshire; and designer, illustrator, and cartoonist Peter Bramley, of New York City. If this book has a broader perspective on silversmithing than could possibly be reached by one silversmith writing in a vacuum, it is to the credit of these my artisan friends; if there are inaccuracies despite our collective efforts, that responsibility is squarely my own.

I owe a debt of thanks to two members of my family who consented to read the manuscript with a critical eye, and thereby caught a number of howlers that might otherwise have found their way into print: Bertha Hatvary, a veteran editor and patient aunt, and my brother Alex Humez, with whom I have had the joy of collaborating on many literary and artistic projects since we were both children. He and Ms. Hatvary have most ably assisted me in stating some things more clearly than I might have if left to my own devices — though here again, if what results is still not clear enough, that is my fault, not theirs.

Finally I am grateful to Tom Brown for his permission to use his rendering and exploded drawing, reproduced on page 109, of his sterling cigarette humidor; and to Susan MacDougall for her photographs of Tom's work and shop on pages 96 and 120. Except where indicated, all other drawings and photographs are my work; even there, I have been assisted by Alex Humez and Kecia Helberg in the actual taking of photographs.

"You know, Nick, everybody's becomin' a jeweler."

Benjamin Rosenberg, proprietor of
Boston Findings and Jewelers'
Supply until his death in 1973.

The Little, Brown Craft Series is designed and published for the express purpose of giving the beginner — usually a person trained to use his head, not his hands — an idea of the basic techniques involved in a craft, as well as an understanding of the inner essence of that medium. Authors were sought who do not necessarily have a "name" but who thoroughly enjoy sharing their craft, and all their sensitivities to its unique nature, with the beginner. Their knowledge of their craft is vital, although it was realized from the start that one person can never teach all the techniques available.

The series helps the beginner gain a sense of the spirit of the craft he chooses to explore, and gives him enough basic instruction to get him started. Emphasis is laid on creativity, as crafts today are freed from having to be functional; on process, rather than product, for in the making is the finding; and on human help, as well as technical help, as so many prior teaching tools have said only "how" and not "why." Finally, the authors have closed their books with as much information on "next steps" as they could lay their hands on, so that the beginner can continue to learn about the craft he or she has begun.

GERALD CLOW

Contents

chapter
1
Properties and Principles

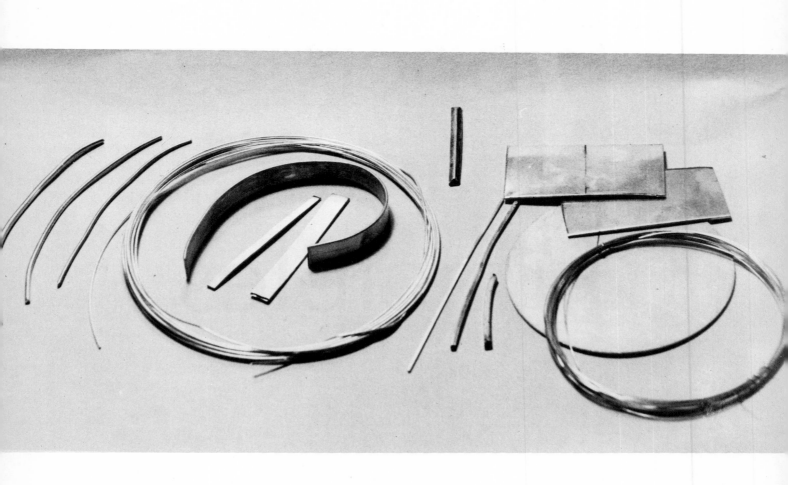

straightedge
compass
drawing tablet
workbench

Bowl with chased ribs, c. 1695;
corrugated trash can, modern.

Silver is a soft, dense metal, easily polished to a mirror finish. In color it is a warmer, yellower white than white gold, platinum or steel, all of which are much denser; aluminum is a paler, bluer white than silver and weighs a great deal less. In the United States and Britain, the standard alloy is 925 parts pure silver to 75 parts pure copper, by weight, and is called *sterling,* variously abbreviated *S.S.* or *Stg.,* or indicated by the figures *925.* Other grades of silver are *Fine* (i.e., 99.9 percent pure) and *Coin* (between 80 and 90 percent pure). The latter was frequently used for flatware in the last century, and the former is still in use for bezel and cloisonné wire to hold stones and enamel. Medium solder, an alloy of silver, copper and zinc, is about 70 percent pure. Britannia standard, on the other hand, was about 95.8 percent silver; from 1697 to 1719 it replaced the British sterling standard, as part of a government effort to keep the nascent Bank of England afloat. Silver as fine as 95 percent is too soft to hold up under stress unless some fancy tricks are resorted to, such as the fluting characteristic of bowls of that period; this fact was acknowledged in the preamble to the 1719 bill restoring the sterling standard. This book will primarily be concerned with sterling silver; *silver,* or *the metal,* should be read *sterling* unless clearly indicated otherwise.

3

Sterling silver is *ductile:* an ingot of silver can be made into a wire as fine as the eye can see. (Gold is a hundred times more ductile yet.) Silver is *malleable:* it can be folded, bent, flattened, coerced, and stretched into a variety of shapes that would be impossible to hammer out of a sheet of aluminum (which is why much aluminum is cast instead). Unlike iron, silver can be worked at room temperature. It stiffens up when hammered or bent (work-hardening); were this not so, you could not make a spoon handle strong enough to resist bending in use. To release some of this stiffness, the silversmith may resort to *annealing* — making the metal soft again by heating it to disintegrate the crystal structure. (See Chapter 4.) Moreover, silver lasts a long time, protected in part by the tarnish which builds up on the surface. Consequently, no self-respecting silversmith ever makes anything he or she would be ashamed to have some archaeologist find a thousand years from now.

Silver is presently between four and eight dollars an ounce, depending on where you go and how much of it you buy at one shot. If you are buying one hundred troy ounces, you will pay closer to four dollars. If you want six inches of 18 gauge round wire, you'll likely pay closer to eight dollars. (Approximately twelve feet of 18 gauge round wire weighs one troy ounce. See Chapter 6 for troy weight and equivalents.) These are about twice the comparable prices two years ago; this increase is due both to the growing number of people making silver jewelry (for fun or in hope of profit) and the devaluation of the American dollar, making precious metals look good by comparison as an investment, adding to the demand on futures (in the commodities market, much as one would speculate on next year's crop of soybeans). As silver is dear, so are the tools to work it, many of which are made in overseas factories and imported, at a substantial markup, by a handful of companies. For these, however, there are often cheaper domestic substitutes, which will be discussed wherever applicable.

If you are new to the arts, you may have heard a lot of talk about design, and may wonder what makes a composition good or bad. This is not a simple question to answer, since what is pleasurable to the senses varies from person to person, and *beautiful* vs. *ugly* can't be verified quite as easily as, say, *wet* vs. *dry*. Nevertheless, there *are* specific sensory experiences tied in with each art form, of which the artist must be aware if he or she is to work in that medium effectively. Here are some of the ways in which we experience a piece of silver.

A. *Texture*. Silver can be hammered in small facets, or polished very smooth, or scraped with hard florentining tools or with gravers, or cast into rough surfaces like charcoal, or struck with beading tools, stamps, chisels, intaglio dies,* or punches. Each of these produces a different texture, and if you are not feeling a piece as you work on it (or if you are not allowed to touch finished work on display), you are missing an important part of the experience.

* A striking tool with a design cut into it, producing a mirror image of the design in relief on the metal.

B. *Weight.* In a world of aluminum, plastic, cloth, and occasional wood, silver is unusually dense by comparison. With both texture and weight, *balance* is the key word: Should a piece be made a little heavy in the handle? Will a ring you are making prove too heavy on top and slide around the finger? Does the pendant you made hang cockeyed? If you use both smooth and rough textures, are they readily distinguishable by feel, and do they seem placed in some kind of order? Hence the question of *visual* balance: if a piece looks off-center, it might as well be off-center since it will be perceived as such anyway. (Here is where preliminary sketches really pay off.)

C. *Reflection.* Silver will take a high polish and reflect like a mirror. Thus the light striking a ring that has tiny facets (instead of a continuous curve) will be scattered, in much the same way that the tiny mirrors in old candle-sconces disperse light from a small source over a fairly large area. To work a piece of silver with a large surface area is a little like designing a Hall of Mirrors for a carnival's fun house.

D. *Conductivity.* Silver feels warm on a hot day, and cold on a cold one. This property can be exploited in the same ways one can use texture, or have to be gotten around somehow, as when the eighteenth-century silversmith mounted carved sections of fruit-tree woods in the center of handles on teapots, spout cups, etc., where near-boiling liquids within would make a solid silver handle unbearably hot to hold.

E. *Heat expansion.* All metals (even the Bureau of Standards' platinum-iridium one-meter bar, down in that insulated pit) expand when heated: the gaps visible between the ends of rails in a train track on a cold day in December are to allow for the expansion of the metal on a hot day in July. The amount by which silver expands is by no means negligible; spokes for a miniature wheel which fit at room temperature will be found to be too short at solder temperature* because

---

* The temperature at which solder liquifies and flows, lower than the melting point of the metal to be joined.

Light scatters from a planished ring

Tankard handle from forked branch.

3-inch cymbal, sterling, by N. Humez

the rim to which they are to be soldered has also expanded. Even the heat of a high-intensity lamp can cause a silver pin with a piece of ivory in it to expand enough for the ivory piece to crack. On the other hand, the difference in coefficients of expansion of two metals *can* be turned to considerable advantage, as in a thermostat where the metals, back to back with one another, expand at a sufficiently different rate to cause the bimetallic strip to bend when heated slightly, breaking an electrical contact. (Circuit-breakers are often made that way also.)

F. *Sound.* A piece of wrought* silver as heavy as half an ounce will ring pleasantly when struck; a bowl four ounces or heavier will produce a fundamental and several audible harmonics, and a set of them can be played like a xylophone or steel drum. (I have seven bowls on which I can play the Ode to Joy from Beethoven's Ninth Symphony, if I choose to do so.) Boilermakers work on even heavier pieces of metal (traditionally copper), hence the sound produced by striking a boiler is deeper and louder, with more harmonics audible, than would be produced by a silversmith working on even a sizeable piece of hollowware. This is why deafness is traditionally associated with boilermaking, not silversmithing, as a significant occupational hazard.

G. *Tarnish.* Silver reacts with sulfur in the air to form silver sulfide, or tarnish. Pieces with high relief will tend to stay bright on the high parts, where most handled, and get darker and darker in the crevices. This natural process may be accelerated, either accidentally (as happens with a silver spoon in a mustard jar, or a silver fork used to eat eggs) or deliberately (with a tarnishing compound like liver-of-sulfur). Anticipating where the tarnish will occur is as much a part of designing a piece as figuring out the balance. (Consequently, when you get a piece in for cleaning that has engraving, relief, etc., try to keep the low parts dark: beware of immersing such pieces in Tarnex or other chemical tarnish removers as they

* Worked and stiffened with hammers, pliers, etc.

7

will remove both the tarnish you want to get rid of and, unfortunately, the tarnish you'd rather keep.) Salt spray seems to tarnish silver rapidly, too; if you are near the ocean, keep silver insulated from the air when not on display, e.g., in Ziplok bags, which can save you hours of polishing with a rouge-cloth.

H. *Function.* Most silver objects made today have a function, aside from their usefulness as works of art. (A theatrical performance or a symphony is useful in that way, too, although the function is on a pretty cerebral level.) Accordingly, the use to which a piece will be put must be taken into account when designing it. Earrings which weigh as much as a tenth of an ounce apiece may prove too heavy to wear for more than a few hours; a ring must be made narrow enough in the shank* that the wearer may still bend that finger. Bracelets must be large enough to fit over the hand, but small enough not to fly off the wrist at the first expressive gesture, and rings have to fit to far closer tolerances yet. Flatware must be angled in such a way that it is not too awkward; a contrary example, perhaps a little extreme, may be found in the diabolically clever spoons made to "cure" lefthandedness, usable only in the right hand, with which the Victorians produced a generation of stammerers. If you make a hot-drink container and give it a solid silver handle, you may well cauterize the eventual user, and (like Jacob) bring upon yourself a curse and not a blessing. I will warn you, in the chapters which follow, of such snares for the unwary as my colleagues and I have fallen into from time to time; I shall do this, not only to save you the bother of making the *same* mistakes, but also to dissuade you from thinking that anybody can become a good silversmith without committing some awful howlers along the road.

How does one become a good designer? Granted, one can be attentive to the strictly mechanical considerations above and still fall short of creating "Great Art." Perhaps I can clarify

* The part of a ring worn in toward the palm.

still further by repeating what one nineteenth-century theorist (John Ruskin, Victorian Britain's foremost art critic) had to say about design:

> Composition . . . means the putting together of lines, of forms, of colors, of shades, or of ideas . . . ; the word being of use merely in order to express a scientific, disciplined, and inventive arrangement of any of these, instead of a merely natural and accidental one.
> ("The Nature of Gothic," *Stones of Venice,* vol. II, ch. 6)

Note that Ruskin says "*merely* natural and accidental." There is no reason why one cannot design a perfectly good piece incorporating an uncut turquoise and randomly fused scrap silver, but they must look as if they *belonged* and didn't just get left there by mistake. (This is very hard to do, and get away with, until you have developed some notions of the conventions of the trade. Although I have been setting cabochons* for years I still do not like to fiddle around with uncut, tumbled stones: like English, it is a difficult tongue to speak well.) Note, too, the word *inventive*. The whole point of copying great masters is to develop your own ability to handle the medium in which you work, and therefore to express your own ideas, not somebody else's, and the sooner you graduate to doing your own designs the better you will feel — I guarantee it. Peace symbols, zodiacal signs, and other nametags that designate membership in groups or organizations (such as fraternity pins, etc.) are mostly a waste of time — although, as much retail silversmithing work is of a commemorative type, each case must be judged on its own merits.

How does the artist come to figure out what his or her best version of "scientific, disciplined, and inventive arrangement" is? How, in short, does one design, and what is one really *practicing* when one is learning to be a good designer? I asked four of my colleagues (two from formal design-school backgrounds and the other two self-taught). Here are my notes on their replies:

* A stone cut in a dome with a flat bottom, either oval or round.

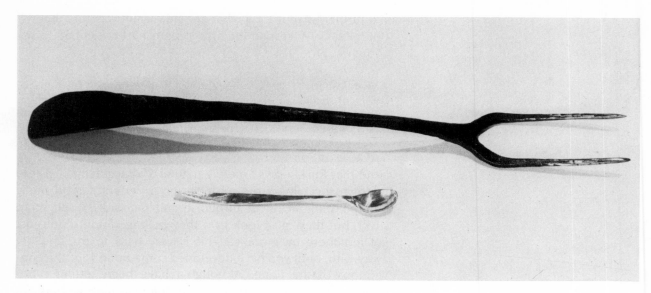

Iron fork and sterling spoon, by T. Brown

Douglas French: "Quality" is a concept not confined merely to making jewelry or any single activity, but is an approach to life generally, and consequently manifest in whatever one does. (Ruskin, elsewhere in "The Nature of Gothic," repeatedly stresses the concept that in whatever ages artists were free or servile, their art shows it, a related phenomenon.) In the broadest sense, if you do not love your art, or if you do not take it seriously, you will never do a good piece in your life; but *quality* goes far beyond that. It is closer to the idea of *being committed,* the sort of bond for which it is reasonable to be vilified, thrown in jail, or shot for a just cause. It is the same "quality" as in the phrase "quality of life": if you do not strive for it, you will look back and discover you have wasted your time. (See Pirsig's *Zen and the Art of Motorcycle Maintenance* for a fuller treatment.)

Tom Brown: All other things being equal, the simpler design is the better one. The more parts there are in a given piece of work, the more are likely to break. The most striking difference between amateur and professional jewelry is that the pro knows when to stop.

The greater your command of materials and tools, the wider your repertory of design will become. Hence the greatest growth will come about when you do a lot of work with an unfamiliar tool, or a new stock, or when you try out a new technique. (Tom's recent application of blacksmithing technology to heavy silver is a case in point.)

Michael Moore: It's trial and error, mostly. You get an idea, file it away in your memory, and then later, when you're doing something, just zing it right in there.

Peter Bramley: Monkey around with everything.

Whatever you do, you will want to learn as much as you can about your materials and tools in order to use them intelligently; and just as knowing how to read is the key to doing scholarly research, so drawing is the first tool, the tool of tools, to designing. It does not matter if you draw well, or prettily; the important thing is that you draw everything — from landscapes with arches, to rings in a ring-case, to how the pistons work on a steam pump — that you think might possibly come in handy later. Your sketch pad is a visual notebook, and just as you become proficient in writing mostly by writing a lot, so the more you draw the better your drawing will become — and, more to the point, so will your silversmithing. Another good reason for always carrying a sketchbook is that you often get your best ideas in unlikely places — on the streetcar, or at the lunch counter, or someplace away from your drawing area in the shop — and by the time you get back to your drawing board the idea is lost. A sketchbook can be a treasury of ideas, yours and others, so that whenever you are doing a piece and need a bright idea you can go to your sketchbook and (as Michael Moore so aptly put it) "zing it right in there."

The right drawing pad is the one you feel comfortable with. I draw on a fanatically small scale and have gotten by for years with a 4" x 6" Strathmore drawing pad, spiral bound; Tom Brown, on the other hand, would be horrified to have to work on anything smaller than 18" x 24". As a result, my drawing pad is infinitely more pocketable than his, but his drawings are undoubtedly more lucid. Suit your own tastes.

Three words of caution, before we get down to brass tacks. First, watch out for the buffing wheel: it is a dangerous tool in the hands of the unwary, and should be respected/feared as much as a power saw. Therefore, if you get access to such a machine and are tempted to use it immediately, *read Chapter 5 first,* where I explain how to use the buffing wheel without losing a finger, an eye, or worse.

Second, choose your work space and bench sensibly. Bear in mind, for example, that you will be hammering on metal, so make sure you don't set up shop directly beneath somebody who's trying to study or sleep during your work time, or who is just plain easily provoked. (This goes for all four sides and downstairs as well.) In addition, a well-ventilated room is a good idea, since your torch will draw oxygen out of the air in the room and it is well to have plenty to go around. (I will say more about shop design in Chapter 12.) The best workbench should be solid, though any table will do, provided it's not too rickety: small objects will be held against it or clamped to it, and you want them not to wiggle around too much while you are working on them. My present bench is a metal-topped table; since liquids will be spilled on it, this prevents the wood tabletop from damage, and from catching fire as well on those rare occasions when a piece of hot silver rolls off the asbestos soldering area. My previous bench, a converted drafting board, I partly sheathed in 36 gauge copper, much as used to be done in shipyards to protect the hulls of frigates from sea worms.

Third, a word about attitude, or *where your head is at.* When you sit down at the workbench, if you are not prepared to commit yourself to being *all there* — not thinking about lunch, or where the rent is coming from, or why so-and-so is peeved at you, or even how groovy you are sitting at this workbench — you are doing yourself and the metal no favor and will probably botch the job in front of you, possibly exposing yourself to danger as well, should your torch or buffing wheel malfunction. Similarly, if you are furious at the world and take it out on the silver, your problems will not go away and your work will probably lack subtlety, even if your aim is good. And if you are just plain sloppy, your work will show it, and in a soberer moment you will be ashamed to have wasted your bench time so. To a certain extent, you will smith silver with the same style with which you run the rest of your life; hence "cleaning up your act" on the bench — that is, trying to do as good a job of *being* a silversmith as you know how — will work or not work according to how well you are coping with the world outside the workshop. Don't hope to do your best piece the day after your cat dies: it is simply too much to expect of yourself.

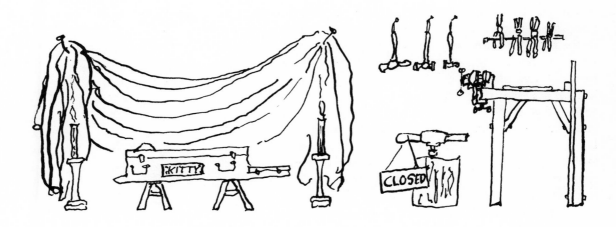

chapter

2

Fire
and
Fusing

torch (propane or acetylene)
asbestos soldering pad
pickling solution (Sparex)
Pyrex bowl
6-inch steel crosslock tweezers
6-inch copper or brass angle-tipped tweezers
4-inch steel fine-pointed straight tweezers
small vise
benchpin and block
jeweler's frame saw
12 sawblades (00 or thicker)
chain-nose pliers
diagonal cutters
2 half-round needle files
riffle file
soldering stylus
5 feet of 16 gauge round wire, sterling
2 blocks of casting charcoal
hot plate (optional)

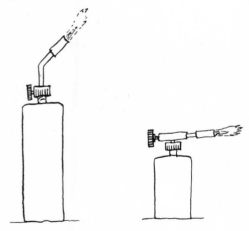

Quart and pint propane torches.

The first order of business for any metalsmith is a heat source, ideally hot enough to melt fairly large quantities of the metal quickly, and therefore more than hot enough for welding (which requires only that the *surfaces* of the two pieces to be joined should be molten). The two gases most commonly burnt in silversmiths' torches are propane and acetylene. The Bernz-O-Matic propane torch comes in both quart and pint sizes; the head on the pint ("Bantam") torch is at a better angle and the torch weighs a lot less than the quart-sized one, but two cylinders for the Bantam cost 25 percent more than one quart tank. (Clearly you are paying for packaging.) You can get either Bernz torch and a couple of refills for under twelve dollars at a discount-store hardware department. By comparison, the "MC" size Prest-O-Lite torch (Union Carbide's acetylene rig) costs sixty or seventy dollars, which is why every silversmith I know, myself included, started with a propane torch.

Operating a Bernz torch is simple. Screw the nozzle attachment onto a cylinder, hand-tight. Open the valve (by turning the knob) with one hand while striking sparks with a sparker in the other, about an inch in front of the nozzle. The gas should ignite in a second or two; adjust the flame size by opening and closing the valve.

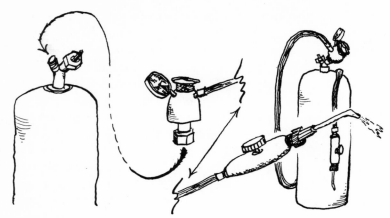

Prest-O-Lite acetylene rig: (left to right) tank, regulator, handpiece, and assembled torch

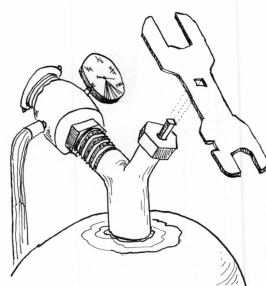

Prest-O-Lite: main valve

18

The Prest-O-Lite torch is a little more complex, but not much. The tank has a V tube on top, one side of which is a threaded valve-seat and the other is a hexagonal nut (*hex-nut* for short) with a square pin sticking up through a hole in the middle. The threaded side is for the regulator, to be tightened on with your tank wrench (you will be sold one with the tank). *After the regulator is attached,* the square pin on the other side should be turned a quarter-turn to open the tank valve. (There is a square hole on your tank wrench for this purpose.) This valve should always be turned off when you leave the shop, as any accident to the regulator in your absence — such as the tank getting knocked over and the regulator snapping off — turns the tank into a rocket, a heavy cylinder propelled by escaping gas capable of crashing through walls and devastating anything in its path, to say nothing of the risk of explosion. Better to play safe and turn the tank valve off when you are not in attendance.

The first time you open the main valve on a new tank, test for leaks. (You get a full tank every time you turn in your empty one, but it's usually not the same tank you walked in with. Thus you always own *a* tank, but never any tank in particular — a curious twist on the notion of "ownership.") Put soapsuds on the hole around the square pin; if they froth or bubble when the valve is open, tighten the hex-nut beneath. In all likelihood your tank wrench will not have a slot the right size: Union Carbide doesn't want to make it *too* easy for the consumer to let a whole tankful of gas escape through the valve by mistaking it for the nut on the bottom of the regulator. You may get around the manufacturer's questionable prudence by putting a nickel next to the valve nut and fitting the next slot up on the wrench over both. Otherwise your only recourse is to take the tank all the way back to the welders' suppliers and have them tighten the valve nut. If the leak does not stop when you tighten the valve nut, close the tank down and take it back: the valve is probably shot and you wish to take no chances with faulty equipment and explosives.

It is a good idea now and then to check for leaks at other points on your torch as well.

The regulator has a valve on the side with three letters (*A, B,* and *C*) in broad diamonds, visible on the side of the fat threaded column. This valve is closed when it is screwed all the way out, and *should* be closed if you are leaving the torch for more than ten minutes or so, in case either the handpiece or the hose springs a leak in your absence. For a working pressure of 5 p.s.i. (pounds per square inch), open the valve by screwing it in until the diamond *B* on it is half covered; *C* is 10 p.s.i. A No. 2 tip in the handpiece will work fine at 5 p.s.i.; you may want to increase the pressure to 6 or 7 p.s.i. (between *B* and *C*) for a larger tip.

The knob on the handpiece valve controls the actual size of the flame, and should be turned off when the flame is not lit. The tip screws into the handpiece, and the holes at the base of it allow the air to be sucked in through the handpiece in proportion to the pressure of the gas, resulting in a hotter

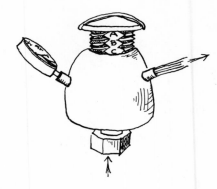

Prest-O-Lite: regulator

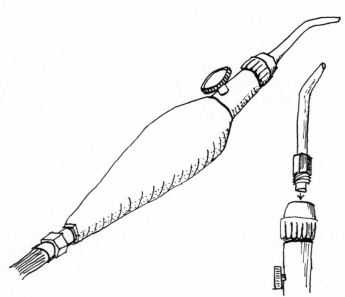

Prest-O-Lite: handpiece and tip

flame than a nozzle with no draft. I find a No. 2 tip quite adequate for most jewelry work, but I switch to a No. 3 or even No. 4 for heavier pieces, or for annealing. At last notice, Union Carbide had discontinued the No. 2 in favor of the No. 1A, which is too small; but Airco makes a No. 2 also.

To shut down a Prest-O-Lite entirely, close the tank valve first, *tightly*. Then open the handpiece valve to bleed off all the gas in the regulator: do this in a well-ventilated area, and *no smoking*. As the gas in the regulator escapes, the pressure-gauge needle will drop to zero; a couple of seconds later, the hiss of the gas will die away. Then close the handpiece valve (and the regulator valve, while you're about it). The regulator may now safely be unscrewed from the tank.

Oxy-acetylene and oxy-propane torches bear mention as well: instead of air (which is only 20 percent oxygen) being drawn into the nozzle by the draft created by the pressure of the escaping gas, pure oxygen under pressure is allowed to mix with the gas at the handpiece. A far hotter flame results: oxy-acetylene, for example, is commonly used to cut or to weld steel — much more heat than is necessary (or desirable) for silver.

Other heat sources include the alcohol lamp and blowpipe, the usual tools for small soldering jobs in the eighteenth-century shop, still extensively used overseas. For larger work the silversmith had a forge as well, a furnace fired by wood or charcoal and fed air by a bellows. While the blowpipe produced small, localized hot spots on otherwise cool work, the forge would heat the whole piece; thus it was used for annealing and to melt silver for casting. In addition, it served to heat iron for tools, since the eighteenth-century silversmith had to make most of his own and therefore had to be part blacksmith as well.

Having gotten a torch, you will also need a square of asbestos (solid rock or press fiber) as a soldering pad. My favorite size is twelve inches square; you can also buy them six inches on a side, and Tom Brown likes to have three or

Small corner forge (windows are covered so that glowing metal can be seen at its true color)

four of these so that he can arrange them as the job requires (6 inches x 18 inches, for example). You will also need a can of Sparex, or equivalent pickling agent. Both this and the asbestos pad are available from any jewelers' supplier. You will also want a Pyrex casserole dish (the five-and-ten should have this) to hold the pickling solution.

To handle the metal while it is hot, you will want to have at least three pairs of tweezers: a reverse-grip, to hold stick solder or other small objects; a long pair with angled tips, for fishing objects out of the pickle; and a short pair with fine points for all soldering work. You will eventually want more of the last type, since they get too hot to handle and a spare of the same sort saves waiting for one pair to cool or using your fishing-out tweezers. Angled tweezers *should* be copper or brass to avoid being corroded by the pickle, but I have used a steel pair for years and they are far from eaten away.

Benchpin

Fine-pointed tweezers eventually soften in the heat; the points can be restored by judicious filing.

Get a small vise whose jaws are under 3 inches wide. (Any hardware store will have this.) Mount it on your workbench; mine is immediately to the right of the soldering area. On the left I have a steel block and benchpin, one unit, and you should acquire one of these too, even if your jewelers' supplier has to backorder it. For one thing, the benchpin serves as a backstop against which to brace any work to be filed that can't readily be worked while clamped in the vise (the inside edge of rings, for example). This is especially true if you saw a V in the end of the pin, since you may then rest work on the two prongs of the fork while filing or sawing the middle. For another thing, the block of the benchpin, properly polished, will do for an anvil until you invest in a proper one (Chapter 4), and for a surface plate* thereafter. Moreover, if you put your benchpin immediately to the left of the soldering area, you can rest your elbow on it while holding the torch, as I do.

For hand tools you will need a jeweler's frame saw and a dozen blades (00's are my favorite, but if you buy thicker ones no harm will come of it, and 00's do break easily), two 6-inch half-round needle files, a pair of diagonal cutters, and a pair of chain-nose pliers. These last differ from ordinary needle-nose pliers in having smooth jaws — teeth would scar the work — and the best ones are box-jointed, not side-jointed like the cutters. With the exception of your torch, all the tools mentioned in this chapter may be bought for a total of twenty-five or thirty dollars; while you are at the jewelers' supplier, pick up five dollars' worth of sixteen gauge round wire, sterling, which will amount to about five feet.

Mix enough pickling solution to fill the Pyrex casserole two-thirds of the way up. Most silversmiths I know keep the pickle-dish on a hot plate set to 150°F or so. After a piece of silver is heated in the soldering area, it must be quenched: most silversmiths plunge it into cold water and then pickle it, but I

---

* A steel plate with a flat surface against which other work can be formed flat also.

use the heat of the silver directly in the pickling operation by quenching the piece in the Sparex dish; accordingly, I do not heat my pickle otherwise. (This is in line with the Principle of Greatest Simplicity put forth by Tom Brown back in the section on design.)

A second dish, with water in it, should be kept handy to the pickle-dish for quick rinsing of work that has just been pickled: you will find this easier than getting up from your bench to rinse all your work in the kitchen sink, especially when several stages of soldering are necessary. Keep paper towels handy: Sparex disintegrates cotton fiber (especially denim), and towels used for Sparex spills, or even for drying silver from a slightly contaminated water-dish, will fall part in six months.

Silver has a high surface tension (as does mercury) in its liquid state. You can see this yourself by the following experiment. Cut some short pieces (two inches or so) of 16 gauge round wire. If you lay one of your sticks down on the asbestos, and direct the flame of the torch at one end of it, you will see the whole piece begin to glow red in five or ten seconds; then the hotter end will brighten and begin to melt, first just on the surface, then deeper. As the end melts, it forms a ball, and the ball starts to crawl back up the solid part of the stick: here surface tension has overcome inertia. At this point, direct the flame of your torch elsewhere on the soldering pad; when the piece stops glowing (in this case, almost immediately) pick it up with your angle-ended tweezers and drop it into the pickle-dish. The pickle will sizzle and spatter slightly (which is why I said only two-thirds full, not all the way to the top). Rinse the stick and repeat the process on the other end.

A second method is to set up your torch on the bench so that the flame points into the air directly over the soldering pad. With your reverse-grip tweezers, pick up another 16 gauge stick, and hold it so that the free end is right at the hottest part of the flame, a little in front of the point of the visible cone of flame. (You may determine the precise point by moving the stick along a line from the point of the flame

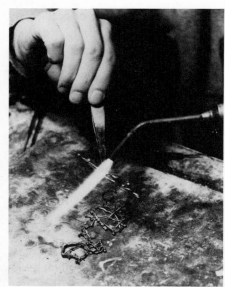
Fusing scrap silver

to two or three inches directly in front of it, and seeing where the silver glows hottest.) If you hold the wire at the hot spot, the end will ball and actually crawl *up* the shaft: up to a certain weight, the surface tension of a blob of molten silver is actually stronger than the pull of gravity. For your own information you should see how big the blob can get before it drops; when it falls to the asbestos pad, quench it immediately.

Finally, you will also wish to try fusing two sticks of silver together, melting their surfaces next to each other so that they join and remain one piece when the molten silver resolidifies. Here again, all silver that leaves the soldering area hot should do so by way of the pickle-dish. If you follow this rule you will keep discoloration of the silver to a minimum.

Charcoal casting is a method of reproducing a design in low relief on a flat background, with the same advantages and limitations as would be entailed in designing the bas-reliefs of winged bulls, gods, heroes, and allegorical figures commonly used to ornament public buildings. Castings in a charcoal mold may be incorporated in anything from tiny studs for earrings on up to a full-sized ring half an inch wide; this method is particularly good for signets for seal-rings. It does not require elaborate equipment; and if you are limited by one side of the casting being flat (in rings, the inside), the clarity of detail which can be reproduced in a good casting more than makes up for this.

You will need two blocks of casting charcoal and a riffle file, both available from your jewelers' supplier. The charcoal should be fairly hard: if you scratch the end of the block with your thumbnail and the charcoal easily flakes and powders, it will be almost impossible to carve and probably will burn as you are trying to cast with it. Do not get saddled with inferior charcoal if you can help it: there may be some *other* use in the trade for soft, powdery charcoal, but I have yet to find out what it is.

The riffle file should be straight-sided with a squared-off heel, as shown. There are lots of other riffle files, but this is the best for scraping down the surface of the charcoal block: the sharp angle of the side and heel makes it possible to get cleanly into corners.

To scratch the actual relief, once you have scraped the surface down, you will need some sort of stylus. An excellent one may be made from an ⅛ inch dowel about three inches long, with the eye end of a darning needle firmly jammed into one end. Mine are cannibalized from an old dissecting kit for biology students, which also included an excellent little pair of pointed scissors quite suitable for cutting thin silver sheet. My stylus, incidentally, does double duty as a soldering tool, as will be seen in the next chapter.

To cut the mold, first spread some newspaper: there will be a lot of charcoal dust, and if most of it makes it no further than the newspaper, cleaning up afterwards will be a great deal easier. Scratch the outline of the piece on the top of one of the blocks. Circles may be marked off with a pair of di-

viders, or with a compass if you use the pencil point as the pivot. (Templates from seemingly unrelated fields may be useful; I use a Sprague template entitled "Logic Symbols for Integrated Circuits." Check your stationery store.) Use the stylus to deepen the outline to the thickness of a penny. Then take the surface down to that depth with the riffle file: lower the edges first, scraping the center down to match, since it is at the edge that you may most easily see how far down you are into the block. Keep blowing the charcoal dust away from the mold, so you can see what you're doing. After you have taken down the surface for the blank, carve your design into it; this will appear in relief, and backwards, so if there is any lettering or right-left distinction remember to carve its mirror image. If the only available charcoal is soft, it may still be carved with a very light touch, but the first casting had better be good since the mold will probably not outlast it.

Set the block with the mold face up on your asbestos pad.

Pile enough silver on top to make the casting, and a little extra. (I save all my clean scrap* for this purpose.) Have your pickle and water set up, and have the second charcoal block handy to your right hand. Light your torch, and heat the metal right on top of the mold (the quicker the better, since prolonged heat will affect even the hardest charcoal, and the soft stuff will glow and turn to ash before your very eyes). When the silver is all molten and begins to dance around, coax it back into the hollow of the mold if it has begun to stray; then take the heat off, and just at the moment when the blob starts to settle down — but before the surface starts to resolidify — slowly but firmly press the molten metal down into the mold with the other charcoal block in your right hand. If you move too suddenly, the high surface tension of the molten silver will cause it to spurt out the side, leaving not enough metal in the mold for your pressure on the upper block to do any

* Scrap which has not been contaminated with solder.

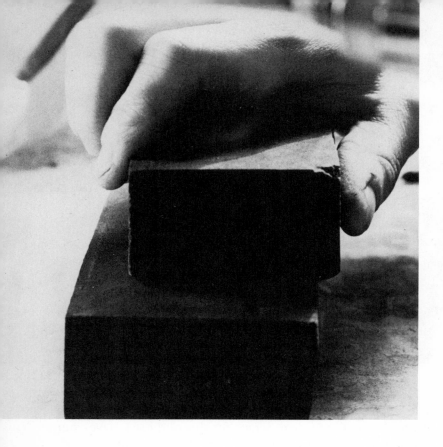

good. If, on the other hand, you wait too long before coming down with the second block, the metal will have cooled to the point where you don't get any detail to speak of. The ideal consistency is a sort of *slushy* feeling — you may readily sense this through the top block. (I put a slight twist on my right wrist as I come down with the second block, which tends to squeeze the sprue* thin, so it is easy to remove afterwards. In bowling this is usually called "English.") The main thing is to force the hot metal into the mold, and *keep it there* until it solidifies, by leaning on the top block for fifteen or twenty seconds. (If you have no watch, or if it's in your pocket where you can't see it, count out loud: "One poor bastard,

* The flashing of extra metal at the openings in a mold left after a casting.

two poor bastards" and so on: this will take you roughly as many seconds as you have poor bastards.) Then remove the top block.

The back of your casting should tell you how good the front is. If the whole mold has been filled (and then some), and the detail of the wood grain from the top block is clearly visible on the back of the casting, the front is probably good too, and the casting can be pried out of the mold with tweezers and quenched in the pickle. If, on the other hand, the casting has a hole in it, and no detail, either you didn't use enough metal to begin with, or you expelled too much of what you did use out the sides by coming down too hard and fast with the top block. Add (or replace) metal, melt it again, and repeat the process.

Removing a casting from a charcoal mold usually breaks off little pieces of the mold, so if the casting doesn't look good on the back, don't try to remove it: fuse the metal again, since the mold is probably still sound, at least, and after one faulty casting you will likely have some idea of how much metal is needed. If you have used too much, the excess can be separated from the main blob by pinching it off the side with tweezers when the metal is just beginning to remelt. Ideally, though, you should get a clear casting with a thin sprue off to the sides.

To clean off the sprue, use your cutters; then file (on the forward stroke only!) to smooth the edges. You may well want to fix the position of the casting in your vise while you work it, rotating and reclamping as you work your way around it. If your sprue is thick, you can saw it off: for this the work must be clamped. Tighten the sawblade into the slots on the frame with the teeth pointing towards the handle: unlike a wood saw, a jeweler's saw cuts on the backstroke. After securing the top setscrew at the right length for a sawblade lying in the two grooves of the bottom setscrews, tighten one of them on the blade (holding the saw upside down with the handle toward you). Now hold the handle against your chest and bow the saw in slightly so that the blade lies further back in the free

Bad casting — metal too hot.   A good casting: back . . .

. . . and front

32

setscrew groove; tighten the screw and the blade is secure and under tension. Release the screw after using the saw so you don't warp the frame.

Sawblades break easily; this is almost invariably due to sudden binding up in the work, which can be minimized by waxing the blade with paraffin, beeswax, or soap. If you keep your saw straight in the cut, it is less likely to bind; and the shorter the cut, the better. Thus a sprue on a round casting can be sawed off in sections by making four or five cuts from the outside of the sprue to the edge of the casting proper, then sawing between them section by section. But even the best jeweler can break half a dozen sawblades in an afternoon without even trying, so be thankful they're cheap.

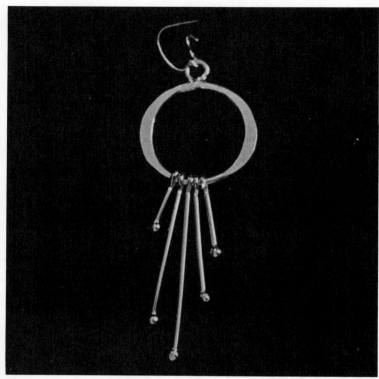

Earring with fused clappers, by D. French

If you want to drill a hole through your casting, mark the position and make a dent there with a centerpunch; this will enable the drill bit to seat itself quickly rather than wandering all over the place. A No. 65 bit should be used for 20 gauge or smaller; a No. 59 for 18 gauge. Like sawblades, drill bits last longer if you wax them.

chapter
3
Soldering

paste flux
liquid flux
spray bottle
2 small brushes
yellow ochre
rawhide mallet
1 oz. medium wire solder
½ oz. medium sheet solder
2 feet hard wire solder (optional)
2 feet easy wire solder (optional)
soldering tripod and screen (optional)

Soldering is the joining together of two pieces of metal by flowing solder into the joint between them at a temperature high enough to melt the solder but not melt the metals to be joined. *Hard-soldering* (brazing) makes a strong joint. The "medium" silver solder which I use is 70 percent silver, and hence bonds readily to 92.5 percent (i.e., sterling) silver; the solder flows at 1390°F, or only 250° less than the melting point of sterling. The strength of joints soldered with low silver content solders like "Easy-flow 3" (50 percent silver), or with lead solders, is sufficient to hold, if not to withstand much stress: low temperature solders are very useful for attaching ear-clips, tie bars, or spring-rings, where a solder requiring higher temperatures would take all the bounce out of the silver (see the section in Chapter 4 on annealing). For structural work, the actual building of the object in silver, a hard solder is to be preferred whenever possible: As a rule I use 70 percent solder wherever possible, and that is most of the time when one is building a piece from scratch. When I was first learning to use a torch, I was told, "The last place a ring should break is at the joint." All my subsequent experience has borne this out: a good hard-soldered joint is the strongest part of the work.

You have already seen how pieces of silver may be joined

by fusing adjacent surfaces, and by now probably have a pretty good feel for how much heat is necessary to do this without overdoing it. Solder temperature should be a little lower — higher than the 1390° at which the solder flows (so that when it is touched to the hot silver, it will flow almost immediately), but not by much. Above 1500° the internal crystal structure of sterling breaks down, leaving the silver fit for little else besides casting. Silver at 1200° glows a dull red; at 1400° a cherry red; at 1500° an orange red; and at 1600° a light orange. (The same holds true for brass, the various trades of gold, and iron and steel.) Hence you may gauge the temperature by watching the color of the metal as it heats.

Silver solder usually comes in coils of 20 gauge wire, or in thin sheet. Since the color of solder and of sterling is about the same, you would do well to mark the solder to avoid confusion: by writing *solder* in magic marker on the sheet, and by crimping the free ends of wire solder in a distinctive way. (I put a right-angle bend on mine.) Failure to do this may result in your trying to solder together a lot of jewelry itself made of solder, as actually happened to a silversmith acquaintance of mine one morning when he arrived at his shop a little bleary; it is to his credit that he succeeded, as, technically, he was welding the solder to itself (rather than brazing) — a far more difficult task than he had bargained for.

To prepare silver for soldering (and, properly, for fusing as well) a *flux* should be applied. Flux serves a double function: as it is heated, it pickles the metal much as Sparex does; second, as its water base boils away, it coats the metal with a glaze which protects the surface from *fire-scale* (the formation of copper oxide on the very skin of the metal, resulting in dark patches which must be abraded off afterwards). Any area that has been fluxed will accept the flow of silver solder. A method of limiting the area into which solder may flow, by using yellow ochre, is discussed later in this chapter.

Flux comes either as a white paste or a liquid, usually dyed green. Either may be applied with a brush; liquid flux can be sprayed onto the metal as it heats. (Brushes eventually fall

Spraying flux

apart from singeing.) A leftover bottle sprayer for window cleaner works about as well as the commercial plant-spraying bottle ($1.50 or so at a hardware store) but holds a lot less. On the other hand, paste flux can be applied to cold metal with bits of solder stuck into it, which is handy for complicated soldering jobs requiring two hands. A second advantage to cold-fluxing is that the application of the flux may knock asunder the various pieces laid out for soldering, and it is a lot easier to put them back where they belong when the metal is cold. Each method has its advantages, depending in large part on how you are going to apply the solder.

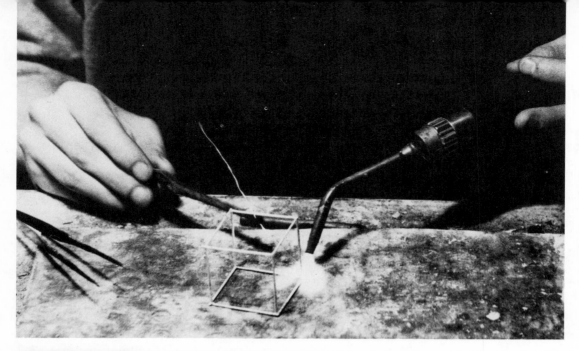

Soldering with wire solder

Soldering with probe and solder snippets

There are three main ways to get the solder into the joint. The commonest is to cut a short stick of 20 gauge wire solder — three inches or so — and grab it at right angles with a crosslock tweezers. Having fluxed the silver, heat it with the torch, as usual, in the left hand, holding the tweezers with the solder in the right. When the two sides of the joint are evenly heated above a cherry red, touch the solder to the joint: the solder should flow in of its own accord, so don't force it. If it doesn't flow readily, the work isn't hot enough and must either be heated quickly, before the flux glaze disappears and fire-scale forms, or else be quenched in pickle immediately, especially if the problem is uneven fluxing. Spraying the work with more flux at near-to-soldering temperatures may yet save you from having to start all over again, but a better remedy is to make sure the metal is properly fluxed to start with, applying additional flux on the way up to solder temperature — not as an afterthought just before reaching it. In all likelihood, though, you will find that the solder goes right where you want it to with little or no fuss. Once this happens, quickly lay down the crosslocks and with another pair of tweezers pick up the soldered work when it has cooled to dull red — a few seconds at most — and drop it into the pickle.

A second method of soldering is to cut little snippets of wire or sheet solder and lay them down for working storage to the right of your work to be soldered (which is to be fluxed as before). This time, though, you melt the snippets of solder one by one, picking them up on the tip of your stylus or soldering probe, from which you then flow each snippet into a joint. This method reduces the risk of disrupting the work in progress: stick solder can easily jiggle the pieces of silver away from each other at the critical moment. Moreover, cutting the amount of solder for each joint in advance means little waste, no mean consideration if you solder gold by this method. Indeed, the only readily available solders for gold come only in sheet form.

A third variation, especially suitable with paste flux, is the placing of solder beforehand as little snippets stuck to the flux at the joints. This leaves your right hand free either to pull the soldered work off the soldering pad without having to change tweezers, to hold a piece to be soldered perpendicular to the plane of the soldering area, or to correct the position of pieces that wander when the flux heats and bubbles.

One trick, handy for soldering vertical pieces to a generally horizontal array, is *sweat-soldering*. Cut a large snippet of solder, melt it, pick it up on the end of the piece to be added, and pickle it. When this piece is heated with the soldered end down, the solder will flow down into the proposed joint aided by gravity. A good exercise would be to solder a square of 16 gauge wire using one of these methods at each corner

for your own comparison. (If the wire is slightly bent, true it up with a rawhide mallet on the flat steel plate of your bench-pin.)

To get used to soldering in three dimensions, you might try to construct a cube. Build two squares of 16 gauge wire; cut four more lengths of wire slightly shorter than the ones used to build the squares. Solder the shorter wires perpendicular to the corners of one square, or two wires to one square and two to the other. This may be done as described above; another method is to prop one square up almost vertically, leaning it against a charcoal block, so that only one edge is on the soldering pad, and solder the short wires lying flat and butted up against the bottom corners on the square. Repeat with the other square and the two remaining wires. If you solder a perpendicular from the soldering pad, check the angle from a least two sides to make sure that it is a true vertical and not just upright in one axis. Once the verticals are soldered, bend them so that the two sides of the cube will line up; set the cube up so that the joints on the bottom, at or near the surface of the soldering pad, are soldered first. Then solder all four joints, or as many as readily line up. If there must be some adjustment, no harm will come of soldering the joints two at a time with pickling in between.

To solder a tetrahedron (equilateral pyramid), remember that the one piece to be soldered vertically without any guide must be at a 60° angle to the two other pieces — here again, check this from at least two views. (The other three regular solids are left as exercises for the reader.)

Soldering problems. Here are the commonest ones, and how to avoid them. I have touched on the problems that come of inadequate heat: the solder won't flow (and will scale over with impurities if left to cook on the metal), and the flux glaze may evaporate, with fire-scale the likely result. If you can solve the problem by turning up the torch, well and good. The dross which forms on the surface of the solder can be skimmed off with the soldering probe and the rest of the solder will flow into the joint once the insulation provided by the skin of impurities is removed.

Often, however, the problem is that the piece is just too massive to be kept hot enough overall to let you reach solder temperature at a particular joint, the rest of the piece functioning as a *heat sink* through which the heat of the torch is dissipated into the air. Prest-O-Lite torch owners can compensate to an extent by using the larger tip. Bernz torch owners, on the other hand, may have to resort to boxing in the back of the piece with two blocks of charcoal, set with a slight gap between them. This will reflect back onto the work much of the heat that would otherwise be lost. The gap between the blocks should prevent convection currents from forming in the hollow, which would otherwise tend to blow the torch out, and the heat loss from the gap is insignificant.

If your solder won't go where it's supposed to, but forms patches, pickle the work and try again: the surface of the metal wasn't clean, or was inadequately fluxed. *Don't* try to solder the joint anyway: at the least it will be unsightly, and at worst will break easily under stress. Remember, you want the joint to be the strongest part of the work, not the weakest.

On the other hand, to keep solder away from certain areas, such as the moving parts of pin-catches, you will find *yellow ochre* indispensable. Available from jewelers' suppliers as a can of powdery clay, it will form a paste with the addition of a little water, and in this form can be painted on the areas to be kept solder-free in much the same way you would paint on paste flux to promote solder flow. Two words of caution: the paste must be allowed to dry thoroughly before the work is heated, or the remaining water will steam up and the paste will flake like latex paint applied to a filthy wall. The other thing to watch out for is that the ochre and flux must not touch each other: heated in combination, the two form a hard ceramic glaze almost impossible to remove. (In the absence of yellow ochre, blood, I am told, will work to contain solder flow almost as well.)

What if two pieces to be joined are of wildly different

sizes? To a certain extent you can control the heating of both pieces by where you point your torch, but if that doesn't work, you can heat sink the smaller of the two pieces by clamping it with crosslock tweezers. Since this will require the torch to heat both silver and tweezers, the effect is similar to that of giving the weaker team an extra player. It may also help to flow some solder onto the smaller piece beforehand and sweat-solder the joint; this will leave your right hand free, of course, and will save fiddling around with multiple pairs of tweezers. I sometimes pickle such work by dunking the whole assemblage, tweezers and all, in the pickle. This is a lot easier than trying to disengage hot crosslocks from the work while it is cooling, and if the tweezers are retrieved immediately no great harm will be done to them. If you are fastidious, buy brass crosslocks for this purpose.

If you have a number of pieces to be soldered in series — four right angles to make two squares, or pairs of links to a chain — it is possible to hold both solder and picking-up

tweezers in the right hand at the same time. Your thumb and middle finger will do the actual pinching on the pickup tweezers, with the crosslocks and solder held against the palm with the fourth and little fingers. With this method, the solder will be directed into the joint by the action of your wrist rather than your fingers; consequently, you may wish to brace your lower arm against something — I use my vise, conveniently mounted just to the right of the soldering area.

To prop up work that can't be soldered flat, charcoal blocks, iron nails, broken needle files, or virtually anything that won't fuse, burn, or explode at 1640°F may be used. This is particularly helpful on those occasions when the joint to be soldered has to be at the top of a three-dimensional piece whose other joints would be endangered were the remaining joint soldered from any other angle. For work which must be heated from underneath, a foot-high *soldering tripod,* with a coarse-mesh screen on top, will serve to support the work and give ample room underneath for the torch head. (Chemistry labs use the same sort of tripod to suspend bottles of solutions to be heated over a Bunsen burner.)

If your soldering operation takes several stages, the danger of heat used to solder later joints melting earlier ones is very real indeed, and sometimes there is no angle at which this situation can be avoided. In such cases you may resort safely to the use of solders of lower than 70 percent silver content. Use the harder solder for the first set of joints, and the softer (lower-melting, with lower silver content) for the rest: it will flow readily at a temperature well below the melting point of the earlier joints. "Easy" silver solder (a brazing solder which flows at 1325°F) is also useful for soldering silver alloys having a silver content and melting point lower than sterling. "Hard" silver solder is 76 percent silver, flows at a higher temperature than "medium" and is suitable for the first joints in complex soldering operations requiring three sets of joints.

Lead-based solders should be noted also: they flow at 375°F, or less than the fusing point of glass, and thus are useful for repairs or subsequent work on silver with enamel. They are also handy for those instances where greater heat would take the temper out of a finding.* On the other hand, joints so soldered are pretty easily broken with a sudden impact, and lead by itself corrodes silver or gold in time. My personal feeling is that any work which you want to last your lifetime should not be soldered with a lead-base solder; but sometimes you have no choice, and it is usually better that a piece be repaired with lead solder than not repaired at all.

* A prefabricated connector for jewelry, such as stud backs, car wires, spring rings, and sister hooks.

Money clip of fused and soldered sterling wire, by N. Humez

48

chapter
4

Hammer and Anvil

stump
stake-holder with ⅞-inch square socket
anvil stake
ball peen hammer
crosspeen (spotting) hammer
forging hammer
planishing hammer (optional)
steel rouge or bobbing compound
lead block
circular felt buff, 4-inch diameter
steel scriber (optional)
2 feet 8 gauge round wire, sterling
two pieces of ¾ x 5 inch 14 gauge sheet, sterling

Rail anvil

My first anvil was a shoemaker's steel last, inverted and dropped into a hole chiseled into the end of a short log of firewood. Wooden wedges would have served to hold the base of the stake in the hole; as it happens, I used splinters and Plastic Wood (not as good). I ground the toe end of the stake on either side to create a small horn, and ground, filed and sanded the heel for a table. That is a classic example of how you can adapt tools from seemingly unrelated sources to silversmithing. Another variation — common on the West Coast — is the rail anvil. I never had one, but I know several people who have. First you find a piece of well-used railroad track, perhaps on an abandoned and partially dismantled freight spur, or by the side of a line where rails have been replaced. Scrapyards tend to be very interested every time some town pulls up its old streetcar tracks, but you may beat them to the scene and some sections may be short enough to carry away. Otherwise you will need somebody to cut a short piece off for you, preferably between one and two feet long. One end can easily be ground into a horn and notches filed at the sides for spikes. This kind of anvil takes a great deal of grinding and polishing before the top is suitable for working, since in all likelihood it will be scarred and pitted, rusty, and too sharply convex to begin with. On the other hand, once you get it flat and polished, it will keep a finish very well: all those iron wheels with great weights on them have work-hardened your rail anvil to a fare-thee-well, and the *real* danger is denting your hammers.

The steel shoemaker's last was harder than necessary, too, and none too stable considering how I had mounted it. My second anvil was a great improvement: it was anvil-shaped, made of soft chrome-iron, solid though portable (twelve pounds) and cheap (seven and a half dollars in 1969, probably about ten dollars now). Although I used it for the next four years, I was never entirely content with it: being so soft, it would not hold a finish and easily dented, and the silver worked on it, accordingly, usually required a lot of polishing afterwards. (Orthodox silversmiths' stakes and anvils are made of sturdier stuff.)

Be inventive: many common objects can be turned into silversmithing tools in a pinch. The only hitch about improvising is that tools made for the job are usually, if not always, handier for that job than anything you can jury-rig. Improvising may be cheap in the short run, or for an occasional situation not likely to recur soon; but once you have spent hours at the buffing wheel correcting for the pockmarked surface of a cheap anvil, you are certain, sooner or later, to get the idea that a jewelers' anvil stake and stake-holder might not be a bad idea anyhow, hang the expense. On the other hand, some tools you will *have* to make by yourself when no tool suitable for what you want to do can be bought. I have a splendid little dapping punch which some enterprising soul made by filing the tip of a fat four-inch nail, and polishing it to a mirror finish. Making tools has many of the same rewards as making anything else, and in any case you are bound to do it some-time.

Get a stump. The best height is about two feet, and it should be at least ten inches in diameter. Both ends should be cut as closely as possible at right angles to the grain so that the stump will not wobble and the stakes mounted on top of

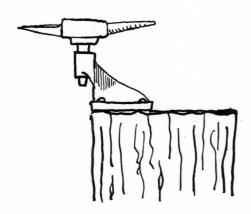

Anvil stake and holder

it will be relatively level. A solid structure of 2 x 4's will serve in place of a stump if the latter is unavailable; some silver-smiths set their stake-holders in a nail keg full of cement, but this has its obvious drawbacks unless you want to remain in your present shop forever.

For anvils you may use any of the alternatives mentioned above, but the handiest by far is the standard stake-holder and stake arrangement. One stake-holder (7/8-inch square socket) and an anvil stake will serve most of your needs, and you may acquire additional stakes at your leisure or as the job requires it. Total cost of these two items is around twenty-five dollars, but they are good steel, the anvil being slightly softer than your average hammer but not dented easily.

If you buy this sort of stake-holder, mount it so that it over-hangs the edge of your stump or bench enough so that you will be able to get at the bottom of a stake held in it, and pop it out of the socket by striking the underside with a hammer. (Keep a plain hammer for this and other mundane use around the shop. *Do not* use one of your planishing hammers, de-scribed below, or you will rue the day.) Remember that you will be working on the top and forcing the stake ever tighter into the holder, so that you must be able to get at the under-side or you will have no way of changing stakes or removing one for polishing except by unscrewing the stake-holder — and *that* should be fastened in with three-inch screws as close to the diameter of the holes along the base of the stake-holder as possible (¼ inch wide). Drill holes in the stump to a depth of two inches where the screws will come through; borrow a bit-brace if you have no power drill, and drive the screws with it as well.

Your anvil stake should be level. You can test this by eye before deciding on the final position of the stake-holder. If your stump is none too level, chisel a level bed for the stake-holder to sit in, and *then* screw it down. (My present stake-holder is mounted in just this way, and has in addition a handle mounted on the side of the stump to carry it to and from crafts demonstrations.)

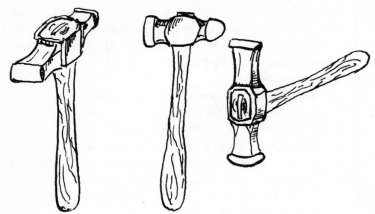

Three hammers: (left to right) forging, ball peen, crosspeen.

You already have a rawhide mallet. You will also need a planishing hammer. I got by for years with a ten-ounce machinist's ball peen (True Temper No. 1504), which like most machinists' hammers is very hard and keeps its shine well, and for the beginning craftsman it is the best deal in town. It has one face sharply rounded and the other only slightly convex. You will also need a hammer with a face curved more than the flat face but considerably less than the ball end of the machinist's hammer; I recommend the crosspeen or spotting hammer, whose opposite face is a polished wedge used in forging and raising. Finally, you will need a forging hammer: it has two wedge-shaped faces, one more convex than the other but less so than the wedge face of the crosspeen. With these three hammers and the rawhide mallet you will be able to do forging, raising, planishing, and some hollowing. You can get by with these four hammers alone for years; I guarantee it.

A cake of steel rouge, a hard felt buff for polishing steel with it, and a block of lead, and you can make flatware, as we shall see shortly.

Planishing is the technique of beating a surface smooth by hammering with hammers of successively less and less con-

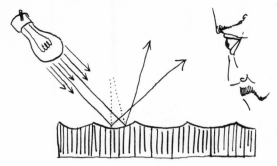

Light is reflected from a surface at the same angle at which it strikes. The observer sees the trough as bright and the adjacent crest as dark. (The dents in the anvil surface have been greatly exaggerated.)

vexity, and with lighter and lighter strokes. This (1) knocks down ridges and dents formed by previous hammer-strokes, fair or foul, and (2) stiffens the metal by work-hardening it (see Chapter 1). In the case of your railroad track anvil, the wheels will have done that already, and indeed such an anvil should probably not be planished as it may already be harder than the hammers. All other anvils, however, are softer than the hammers and bound to get dented sooner or later. Furthermore, when you first buy a stake, its surface will probably want some planishing as they rarely come to you in good shape already, and may even want some filing and sanding (careful!) before you begin to planish. Once the surface is sanded down so that no deep scratches or rust pits are visible (rust will scar your hammers) strike successive overlapping rows, as shown, with as sharply curved a hammer-face as you need to obliterate the existing dents. Do this with a lamp opposite you, so that you can see the ridges clearly. (See accompanying diagram.) Get into a rhythm and let the hammer do the work for you: planishing is *not* the same thing as bludgeoning to death, and no amount of brute force will get you a smooth surface. It is a slow, almost meditative process, and there is no use fighting it. If, on the other hand, your hammer isn't flattening out the dings, use a more convex-faced one, and *then* planish the whole surface. (This sort of spot-work is often called for when you land a really foul shot while hammering silver, and dent the anvil by accident.) After each course, go to a less convex hammer; keep doing this until you have the surface of the anvil smooth to your satisfaction. Then polish it on the buffing wheel using the hard felt buff and steel rouge. Keep your hammers polished with this same rouge and buff. (If you have a planishing hammer one face of which is flat, do not use the flat face as your final hammer on the anvil: even an experienced planisher will stop just short of this, as it only will work if the face strikes *absolutely* flat, with no tilt, which is virtually impossible. Dents made accidentally with this hammer are invariably nasty.)

Granted that planishing your anvil takes at least a good hour's work, it will save you endless hours of polishing or even sanding silver scarred by working on a bad surface. (Try it both ways and see for yourself.) Exactly the same technique is used for planishing silver; hence planishing your anvil is good practice for the real thing.

If you execute a flat design in wire, planishing it will stiffen it; virtually all wire jewelry offered for sale is planished for just this reason, although I suspect that not all of the manufacturers know this, to judge from some of the planishing I've encountered. Indeed, sometimes it appears that they think planishing means pockmarking, guessing that it is a kind of finishing but ignorant of its structural reasons. Thus you will find pieces stretched too thin and brittle in some spots and hardly stiffened in others. This is the mark only of the hasty or ignorant. The *proper* way to planish such a piece is to use as nearly flat a planishing face as you can, and planish the piece evenly and thoroughly. If you want to leave the wire round, only stiffening it a bit, the rawhide mallet will do this.

Annealing means taking the stiffness out of wrought silver by heating it and allowing the crystal structure to break down. Since silver, like any other metal, gets brittle when work-hardened too much (see Chapter 1), if often happens as well that part of a piece requiring much hammering will need to be annealed at least once while it is being worked or the hammers will not be able to stretch it further, even though there is no imminent danger of cracking along the lines of crystallization. To prevent fire-scale, paint or spray the silver with flux while heating it with the torch; heat the metal to a dull red. (Do this, like soldering, out of direct sunlight so that you will be able to see the color-change as soon as it happens.) If the piece is large, allow it to cool for ten seconds or more before plunging it into water or pickle, or the strains you have hammered into the metal will be released all at once, with cracking the sure result. Small pieces cool sooner and can be quenched almost immediately. (Make sure all the flux is off the piece before you planish! Use a Brillo pad or steel wool if necessary; glazed flux is hard and will certainly pit the silver if struck with the hammer, and possibly the hammer face as well.) Your silver should now be soft and malleable as before. Note: if you have an acetylene torch you will need to invest in a larger tip than a No. 2 to anneal anything as large as a table fork. I use a No. 4, which works well on hollowware, too.

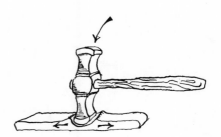

Forging is stretching the metal with the hammers. Note that this can be done with planishing hammers; if you strike only one side of a piece of heavy wire you will stretch that side and compress the other slightly. The advantage to forging hammers is that they stretch mostly in one direction (at right angles to the length of the wedge) with little side distortion. One silversmith I know uses a forging hammer almost exclusively. Others (I am one) use planishing hammers for planishing and some forging, reserving the forging hammer for heavier wire pieces, flatware, etc., where it is really indispensable.

A good exercise at this point: take several pieces of heavy round wire (8 gauge), perhaps an inch and a half in length. Forge these into flat rectangles, doing some with the forging hammer, some with planishing hammers. Planish some of them so that they are flat; you will have to do some truing up

Forging the blank for a fork or spoon

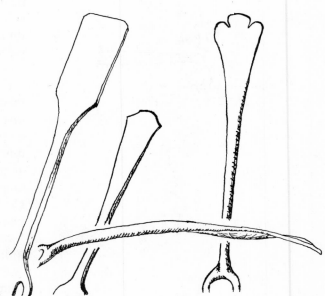

Handle shapes

58

with the hammer on both sides to get them that way. You may also wish to try forging and planishing a curved surface; if so, remember that you need a rounder hammer face for working the inside of a curve, since it is concave to begin with. (Save these pieces for later: broad flat surfaces and curved planes make excellent design elements for the silversmith, as they catch and reflect a lot of light.)

Flatware. Start with the fork. Begin with a piece of sheet stock about two-thirds the width you want the fork to be at the tines. (Here again, drawings help — better to make a mistake with a pen than with a hammer, and only the reckless start in with no idea where they want to end up.) For a small fork this might be ¾-inch wide, as long as you want the finished fork to be, and fairly thick — 14 gauge at least, preferably heavier. (Remember that the thickness goes up as the gauge numbers go down.)

Use a crosspeen or forging hammer to stretch one end of the blank of silver sideways and the other lengthwise, as shown, on the table of your anvil. Then turn the blank sideways and crosspeen the middle of the blank over the horn of the anvil so that the cross-section is nearly square. Work on alternate sides to preserve symmetry; if the blank starts to stretch askew, correct this on the flat table of the anvil and then return to working the sides over the horn. Planish the middle section if it starts to curl in on itself; anneal it if you must (but remember that this part of the fork will bear the greatest strain in use and so has to wind up being hard and stiff). When you have formed the blank to your satisfaction, planish it as you did the previous pieces and your anvil.

Now sketch where the tines will be, marking their position with a steel scriber, or your soldering probe if it is of the needle-in-a-dowel type, on the wider end of the blank. Using the forging hammer, shape the handle-end to taste; several types of handles are shown. The three-lobed type is notched with a saw partway through forging, and then forged some more (this is tricky).

After the handle is forged some (you can do the final forging later if you choose), lay the blank flat across the horn of your anvil just where the tines will end, and bend the blank evenly by striking it with the rawhide mallet. Then turn it over and repeat the process, only a little up the handle (use your favorite table fork for guidance). Then saw the tines out along the lines you have marked, and file their edges round and to a point. File the ends of the tines flat, with a slight slope from the back, as the fork will be a little sharp otherwise. If you want a round cross-section to the middle of the handle instead of a square one, file that also. Then sand all the rough spots and filemarks (your planishing of the fork should have helped this some by leaving as little that needed to be filed as possible). Buff to desired finish; you may want to use a mild cutting compound like tripoli (see next chapter) as an intermediate step in the finishing, and red rouge for the final polish.

Spoons start the same way as forks, although some people suggest a blank wider at one end where the bowl is going to be stretched not only sideways but down into the lead block as well. In any case crosspeen the handle up and the bowl end to the sides, thicken the handle, and planish as before. However at this point it would be a good idea to anneal the silver where the bowl is going to be.

Now take your lead block. With your ball peen hammer hollow out a depression in the block, and shape it with the round face of the crosspeen to an oval. You may smooth the sides by scraping with a pocket knife; make sure no lead is on the blade afterwards, however, before you use it again, as lead is poisonous. (Also wash your hands well after handling lead, for the same reason.) If you have to get the lead into a more convenient form, get an enameled saucepan to melt it on your kitchen stove, and then pour the lead into a mold — pie tin, pipe tobacco can, or any low tin whose bottom is not soldered on (otherwise the solder may melt before the lead solidifies). Never use that particular saucepan for anything else, and do the melting and casting with a good draft, so that

Hollowing spoon into lead block

you will be safe from breathing fumes. It would probably be a good idea to do the pouring over the back of your asbestos pad in case you should spill the lead and in any case to protect the surface underneath from heat. While the lead is cooling, you may try setting the face of the crosspeen hammer flat into it; this will produce a mold as good as you can get by hammering and/or scraping. Heating the top of the lead block in the mold with your torch will melt it enough to make this sort of casting; you need not melt the whole block and recast it.

Lay the spoon blank over the edge of the depression in the lead block, angled into the hole. Hollow the spoon bowl into the depression, starting from the handle end and working towards the front. You'll have to do a certain amount of maneuvering to get the bowl positioned right and hollowed to the proper depth. Try to get an oval bowl shape first; this was commonest in the early eighteenth century, the pointy-ended spoon bowl being a later development. The main thing is to go slowly and use your head, planning each stroke, if necessary: think, "If I hit it *here,* which way will the metal go?" The angle of the hammer face to the spoon blank, and the angle of both to the depression into which you are hollowing the bowl, will determine how the metal will stretch. Watch all three closely. Use light strokes and a lot of them, rather than trying to hollow out the bowl with a single mighty blow.

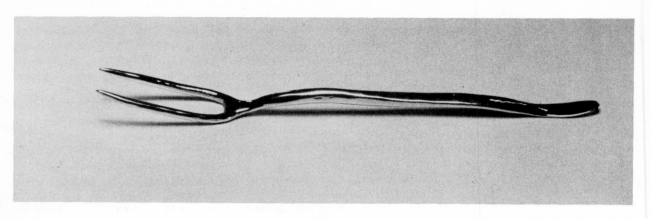

Sterling pickle fork, split and forged, by N. Humez

When you have hollowed out the bowl, it will have a rim around it that will need trimming. Saw the excess off *sparingly* — better to leave extra work for the file (in this case) than to overdo it and get a coffee-spoon bowl on a tablespoon handle. When you have trimmed the rim, file the top flat (in the same plane as your handle). If there is slight skewing — there usually is — correct this with the forging hammer on the handle safely above the bowl before you file the bowl flat. Finally, bend the handle relative to the spoon bowl as you did with the fork; the handle will probably be tilted up anyway and you may need only to straighten it well behind the bowl, so that the handle on your finished spoon goes up at a total angle of ten degrees or so from the flat top of the spoon bowl. Then sand and file to taste as you did the fork, being especially careful to clean off any particles of lead still adhering to the back of the spoon.

Smaller versions of the above can be done using rectangular stock (18 gauge tie bar, ¼ inch wide) thinner than used for full-sized utensils. I have made salt spoons and small pickle forks this way, and it is excellent practice for those who are wary of taking on a full-sized piece right off the bat. Use the ball of the ball peen to do the hollowing. For miniature hol-

62

Sucket fork, eighteenth century

lowware, a riveting hammer or watchmaker's hammer will do for the forging; these hammers are simply smaller versions of the crosspeen or spotting hammer. I use my homemade dapping punch to hollow the bowls.

An ingenious hybrid which you may want to try making is the sucket fork, which has a twin-pronged fork at one end and a spoon bowl at the other, suitable for spearing chunks and spooning syrup from sweet pickles in sauce, preserves, etc. The name probably derives from the French *sucrer,* which means to sweeten with sugar but can also be applied to canning and preserving. I have drawn an eighteenth-century sucket fork, shown from the back so you can see the rat-tail, made by forging the back of the spoon blank in a Y pattern. This was a common design feature of spoons at that time; it not only extended the visual line of the handle well into the bowl, but also strengthened the handle at the edge of the bowl, where the greatest stress occurs in use.

Tongs are another good exercise. If you have no copper pickle tongs as yet, here's how to make a pair. Since copper is about as malleable as silver, you will be able to make silver sugar tongs later in exactly the same way.

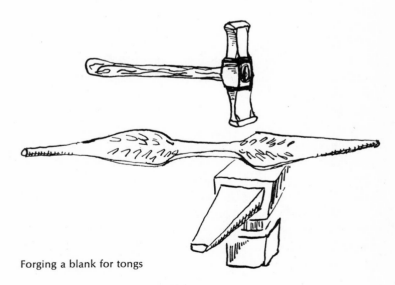

Forging a blank for tongs

63

Start with a piece of copper round wire 8 gauge or so, about a foot long. Forge a "bow tie," as shown; then forge the tips at right angles to make a sort of two-way wedge. Planish, then lay the center of the tongs across the anvil horn, at right angles to the flat handles, much as you did with the spoon and fork blanks. This time, though, forge on one side only, and spread the metal in the middle out as you stiffen the curve. After a bit you will be able to grasp the tongs by the points under the horn, and hold it down against the horn while you hammer on top. The arms of the tongs will probably be of unequal length; snip off the excess to even them up. By a slight modification, you may make crosslock tweezers as well. Joseph Richardson's sugar tongs end in two small spoon bowls; other sugar tongs end in two-pronged forks, rounded claws, or just points. Be inventive.

chapter
5

Finishing

buffing motor (with adapter for buffs)
red rouge
tripoli
2 muslin buffs, 4-inch diameter
chamois buff, 4-inch diameter
liver-of-sulfur and small brush
emery cloth
burnisher (optional)
tumbler and shot (optional)
round, square, triangular and oval needle files
(optional)

*F*inishing," according to Douglas French, "is what separates the real meatballs from the people who know what they're doing." The quality of the finish-work will determine whether the object you have made is "a good idea, as far as it goes," or "a piece that will knock your eye out." Sloppy finish-work will thoroughly undo the best of designs. One reason for this, according to David Pye, is that thoughtlessly finished work assaults us with inconsistent impressions of sight, feel, balance, and so forth. This effect he calls *equivocality;* the following is taken from a chapter so titled in his book, *The Nature and Art of Workmanship:*

> There is . . . a total incongruity and a sense of outrage about a piece of material with a highly polished surface and a raw, rough edge. It is ambiguous in the extreme. Moreover, the tactile implications of what we see are unpleasant. We imagine the soft ends of our middle fingers sliding gently across the smooth surface and suddenly torn open on the raw edge. . . . The effect is quietly barbarous.

If you *want* an air of quiet barbarity, go ahead and do a piece with polish and a jagged edge. But like the uncut turquoise mentioned in Chapter 1, it has to look as if it belonged there and wasn't just accidental. Granted, innovation and unorthodoxy even in this department are part of an artist's stock in trade; still, if you break the conventions of your medium, you had better have it clear in your mind why you are doing it, and whose sensibilities you are about to outrage — a good argument for going to art school. My own experiment in quiet barbarity, the harpoon shown here, is a borderline case of this sort.

In "The Nature of Gothic," mentioned earlier, John Ruskin, maintained that to require an artisan to do precise finish-work is to insist that people become machines. "Never demand an exact finish for its own sake," he said, "but only for some practical or noble end." Ruskin was arguing, and rightly so, against the dehumanization and oppression of the British industrial worker of the mid-nineteenth century. But it is the *mindlessness* of the job that is the critical wrong, not the *meticulousness*. When the artisan has done all the work up to the finishing stages, the work can hardly be said to be meaningless; rather, it is the fruition of the thoughtful design and careful construction of all that has gone before. Surely this would qualify as a noble end — especially if, as I have argued, the *absence* of thoughtful finish-work is so likely to vitiate whatever effect the artisan has so patiently tried to work out.

Ironically enough, the most meaningless jobs in the jewelry industry are to be found in response to the demand for hand-made silver created in part by Ruskin's plea for more *humanistic* craftsmanship: the production houses which specialize in cheap silver jewelry with the "handmade look." Laborers, paid by piecework to ensure maximum production in minimum time, sit at tables with steel tops and treadle-driven hammerfaces, flattening out the curleycues that other laborers, also paid by piecework, have hastily soft-soldered together. Since maintenance on the striking surfaces costs money and takes time, the manufacturers often attempt to gloss over dents and scratches in the hammered work by plating the silver with rhodium. Rhodium does not tarnish, and looks vaguely steely; the effect is a little like that of a marble statue daubed with cream-colored enamel. Proper

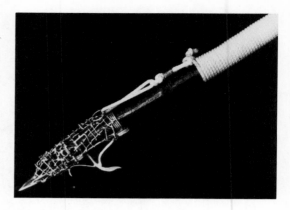

Harpoon, by N. Humez

finish-work takes time and thought, but there is no substitute for it.

Douglas French has justifiably claimed that equal attention must be paid to the finish-work as to all the other stages of design and manufacture combined. It is your last chance to make sure you didn't goof up on the earlier stages: to finish a piece means, of necessity, to inspect it as well. You need not be inhumanly meticulous — Samuel Hopkins Adams's grandfather asserted that "Only a waste-thrift would plane the under side of a privy seat" — just be thoughtful.

Your most important finishing tool is the buffing wheel. This should be a ¼- or ⅓-horsepower electric motor, the shaft of which turns at 3600 revolutions per minute. Some motors have spindles protruding on both sides; this makes it possible to mount two polishing buffs* at once so that one need not switch buffs on the same spindle all the time. One version of this sort of motor uses the left-hand spindle to drive an exhaust fan, which pulls flying dust into a trap behind the right-hand spindle. Even without an exhaust fan, though, it is possible to contain some of the flying debris by boxing in the back of the right-hand spindle with a simple plywood hood. In any case the motor should be mounted — firmly — on a bench in a corner of your workshop where dust is not too critical. (See Chapter 12 for a discussion of separating types of work areas in shop design.)

The motor should be mounted so that it turns towards you from the top, not the bottom — for a right-hand spindle, this means counterclockwise. (Manufacturers usually put the switch on the front of the motor, where it can be easily gotten at in a hurry, so if your switch is *not* in front the motor is probably mounted backwards.) Work caught out of your hands by the wheel will thus be thrown down, not up into your face.

Electric motors of this size usually have a three-prong plug;

* A cloth wheel mounted on a buffing motor to hold abrasives in a tallow matrix.

the third plug is a ground-wire, and is there to protect you from a nasty shock should the insulation of the wiring inside the motor deteriorate. If all your wall plugs are the normal two-pronged sort, buy an adapter at any hardware store: this has three holes on one side, and two prongs and a wire on the other. The wire should be screwed to the center of the wall plate over your regular two-hole plug: the center screw will ground the motor through the building, and not through the artisan.

In all likelihood your motor will have a cylindrical spindle. To adapt it for soft-centered buffs you will need a tapered, threaded cone which fits over the shaft of the motor and is held on with setscrews. Note: these screws are often *Allen-head*, that is, with countersunk hexagonal holes; Allen wrenches are made of hexagonal tool steel stock and have a right-angle bend at one end. (It may seem silly to buy a whole set of these just for attaching one part, but the very fact that they are not much in use around the home or retail store means that they are useful for closing things you don't want just anybody to open, such as glass display cases or light-safes for photographic paper.) Otherwise, borrow one the right size: the tapered cone need never be removed. The buffs thread onto it and stay on due to centrifugal force. Any jewelers' supplier will have such an adapter, or be able to order it for you.

Buy the following, while you are there: a stick of red rouge for *polishing,* and a stick of tripoli for *buffing;* also two sewn muslin buffs, 4 inches in diameter. Tripoli is a fine abrasive, and buffing with it will give you a dull but even network of tiny scratches on the surface of the metal. Red rouge is a far finer abrasive, so fine that the scratches it produces actually average out to an even surface; hence it is classified as a polishing compound. It is now generally thought that buffing is most efficient at a surface speed of 4000 feet/minute, and polishing at twice that; for a 3600 rpm motor, this means a four-inch diameter buff and an eight-inch buff respectively. But you will have your hands full managing a surface speed of

4000 feet/minute as it is, at least until you have gotten used to the machine; and, in truth, you can polish perfectly well at that speed. I have for years, experimenting with different sizes and types (chamois, felt, etc.) of buffs at my leisure. The main drawback, I have found, to using a wide buff with tripoli is that the metal gets cut away too quickly. Buffing should be thought of as the slow, methodical grind; polishing, the quick, vigorous shoeshine. Never switch buffs — would you want sand in your shoe polish?

Silversmithing is not, generally speaking, a dangerous occupation. Although acetylene is explosive, you can take sure precautions against that, as discussed elsewhere. Moreover, the precautions are one-shot: for example, you turn off the tank valve, and it's done.

The buffing wheel is dangerous in another way: the only way not to get hurt is to pay close attention *all* the time the machine is on. Even if the work you were doing at the machine did not command this kind of involvement, your safety does depend on it. If the wheel snatches something from your hands and somehow throws it back at you, that object will be traveling about 45 miles per hour. Thus Tom Brown once narrowly escaped being plugged through the head by his own creation when a pendant he was polishing got caught and thrown; grazing his hair by his right ear, it splintered through a pine-panel wall and across the room behind him to knock plaster off the far wall, a distance of some twenty-five feet. There was a plywood hood on this machine, but an occasional piece eluded capture. Far less dramatic, but far more common, are small flying particles of abrasive that can lodge in your eye. A pair of shatterproof goggles will protect you from this if you don't wear glasses already.

The other chief danger is getting caught. One of my mentors lost a finger that way, and nearly every silversmith I know has his or her tale of woe of trying to buff a chain necklace and getting pulled into the wheel. It is significant that this chiefly happens at the end of the last day before a major holi-

Proper angle for buffing

day: being tired and in a hurry are the two greatest causes of accident with this machine and probably most other machines as well. Of *fatigue*, I would say that there are some things that you can get away with when you're tired, and then there are some you can't, and using a buffing wheel is one of the latter. Hence, if you are tempted to buff something when you are tired (or intoxicated, or taking antihistamines, or just Away), put it off until you are straight. As for haste, finish-work is not to be done hastily. If you have a deadline to meet, give yourself ample elbow-room on the finishing time: quality and your health both require this.

Chain necklaces, wherever possible, should not be polished on the wheel, but tumbled: I will discuss the tumbler shortly. If you absolutely *must* buff a chain (e.g., if you have just repaired one), anchor one end by passing it around a steel hammer. The end of the chain will stay put, and not be caught on the fly; furthermore, if somehow the whole mess gets pulled in anyway, you at least have a handle to pull back that isn't spinning at 3600 rpm. By the same token, secure any part of your clothing (or remove it) that flaps; get your hair out of the way with a hat, net, or elastic; and take off any loose jewelry. This is all part of clearing the decks for action anyway: safety aside, you will be more at ease if the work area is free of obstructions.

Spin a muslin buff onto the motor spindle until it is hand tight. Turn on the motor and apply tripoli to the lower front quarter of the wheel, pivoting the stick of compound against the wheel with your wrists. The matrix in which such compounds are embedded is tallow, which the wheel in effect wipes off the end of the bar. You will immediately feel the pull of the wheel down and back. Be firm; maintain a good grip on the bar of tripoli, and don't follow the wheel: keep the angle shown in the photograph. This is a case where your sense of touch will be worth heeding: too low, and you will feel yourself going under; too high, and the spinning buff will slap you down.

Now take a piece of flatware. Direct each of its surfaces against the wheel much as you did with the end of the stick of tripoli. The tines of forks, the points of sugar-tongs, and any other protrusions should always be buffed point *down*, not up: otherwise the wheel will catch them and throw the piece down. Make the fine adjustments of position with your fingers, but use your wrists for the main pivot, as before. Michael Moore recommends that with flatware, and anything larger, you should hold the piece with a "death grip": since there is a lot to hold on to, you have a handle by which you can restrain the wheel by force if you must. For a small piece, the "breakaway grip" is better: here the object is to have a clear exit for the work, without your fingers getting in the way, should it be snatched by the wheel. This gives you time to duck and turn off the wheel. *Don't* try to chase the piece until you have turned the wheel off: that is *begging* to get caught by the wheel.

One reason people drop things they are buffing is that the heat of abrasion builds up and their fingers start to sizzle. If the piece you are buffing gets too hot, set it down to cool before buffing the rest of it.

Between buffing and polishing, wash the tripoli off the silver. The tallow dissolves readily in ammonia, although plain soap and water will do. Scrub with an old pig's bristle toothbrush (nylon may scratch the silver). Tripoli and red rouge are much more difficult to get out of fabric (once a tripoli buff, always a tripoli buff), so don't wear your Sunday best, or at least wear an old shirt over it. Once you have gotten all the tripoli off the silver, polish the piece in the same fashion using red rouge and the other muslin buff.

To polish steel hammer faces, stakes, and so forth, I use a wider buff (6 inches) and a gray cutting compound called steel rouge; bobbing compound works just as well and most of the silversmiths I know use it instead. Rubber-matrix "Bright Boy" wheels also remove a lot of metal in a hurry. Both of these can also be used to prepare silver for buffing with tripoli, and may, indeed, be the quickest way to remove fire-scale if you

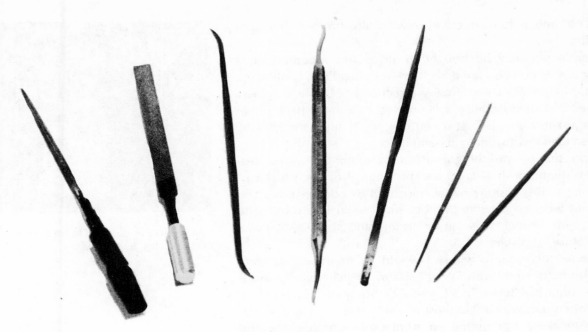

Files and scrapers

are so unfortunate as to have a lot of it. But far greater control is available if you do it with sandpaper by hand: you can see what you're doing before you overdo it. Steel rouge is best reserved for steel.

Tom Brown divides finish-work into four stages. The first is handwork — filing off edges (remember, all files cut on the forward stroke), sanding, and so forth. Note that there are as many shapes of needle file as you could possibly need: square, round ("rat-tail"), triangular, flat on both sides ("equalling"), half-round, and oval, to name the commonest. Of these, the half-round is by far the handiest: I last bought a rat-tail needle file four years ago, and it is still keen, whereas I wear out a half-round in three or four months. When files begin to clog, brush the metal out of the grooves with a toothbrush: this will not only help them cut evenly but also prolong their useful life.

Sandpaper may be bought in strips and mounted on a handle shaped like a large file, for easier handling. (Unlike the files, sandpaper can cut in any direction.) "Flex-i-grit" emery paper, so called because it is bonded to a mylar back rather than a paper one, is best if you can get it, since the backing doesn't fall apart when you bend it.

Burnishing — polishing a surface by rubbing it with a steel tool of high polish — comes at this stage also. The usual burnishing tool is a shiny metal horn in a wooden handle, and should be used for this purpose only when lubricated with detergent. Dental tools can be ground and polished to make miniature burnishers.

Under this same category I would include the deliberate tarnishing of silver with *liver-of-sulfur*. This chemical is available either in solution in a two-ounce bottle, or as a pint-size can of crystals which you must dissolve and mix yourself. For occasional use, I prefer the two-ounce solution: liver-of-sulfur loses its potency on prolonged exposure to air, and once the tin is opened, the days of the crystals are numbered. At my present rate the solution starts running out and going flat at about the same time.

Liver-of-sulfur can be applied with a brush; alternately, you can dunk the whole piece to be tarnished. The silver should turn black in about half a minute, although the process can be accelerated if you heat the piece a trifle, over a candle or a match perhaps. When you have all the tarnish you want, bathe the silver in warm running water to get the rest of the chemical off. When you come to buff the piece, the high parts will reappear as silver while the valleys and crevices will remain tarnished — an excellent technique for exploiting the wood grain in a charcoal casting.

Tom's second division of finishing is buffing, his third, polishing — both done on the motor as described above. Make sure you have thoroughly done the one before proceed-

Cast pendant treated with liver-of-sulfur, with polished relief, by N. Humez

ing to the other: what you miss with tripoli will not vanish with red rouge.

The last division might be called the tying up of loose ends: washing off rouge and tallow, removing tarnish and hand-polishing, the latter two preferably with a jeweler's rouge-cloth for the even, rich shine we know and love in silver. There *are* chemicals that remove tarnish, but they mostly remove good metal too. Pickle does not do this, at least not to the same extent; but then you have to go back to the polishing stage. Nevertheless, I occasionally resort to "Ellanar" silver tarnish remover: sometimes, as in the case of intricate sculp-

Tumbler

tures, there is just no other way to get *in* there with a buffing wheel.

The *tumbler,* although a substantial investment, may prove an invaluable tool at this stage. It consists of a watertight drum in which water, detergent, and steel shot are put, along with the silver; when the drum is sealed and put on its motorized bed to rotate, the steel shot acts like thousands of tiny burnishing tools. If silver with tallow and rouge is put in, adding a little ammonia will get all the tallow out. Moreover, some pieces, by reason of their shapes, may not be easily or safely buffed, chain necklaces and complex geometric figures being examples. (See the tesseract in the hands of the baby at the end of this chapter.) A good cheap tumbler is the Lortone rock tumbler, which cost me twelve dollars in 1972; its capacity is a quart. A larger tumbler (four quarts) with a superior lid (held on by wing nuts rather than vacuum pressure) is made by Scott-Murray of Seattle, Washington, and cost me thirty dollars in 1974.

A few tumbling suggestions:

— You will need about a pound of steel shot ($2.50 a pound in 1974) for a quart tumbler, and three pounds for a gallon one. Make sure the shot is not pitted with rust: you have as much a right to this as not to be sold a rusty, pitted hammer.

— Tumbling time varies with the object: if you are just removing tallow from polished pieces, an hour should do it, whereas it takes upwards of six hours to burnish the insides of the tesseract. Changing the water every three hours gives you a chance to monitor the progress of such pieces.

— If you have more than half a dozen pieces to tumble, string them on a wire, looping the ends securely. This will save you a lot of fishing-out time at the end.

— Silver fresh from the tumbler will still have soap on it and should therefore be rinsed in hot water; spread it to dry on a towel, rather than bunched up on a wire. You may speed this up if you make a sort of sack out of the towel, with the silver in the middle, and shake it vigorously.

— Cover your shot with soapy ammonia water when you are not running the tumbler. This will retard rusting; if you get a *little* rust this can be gotten off by running the shot in the tumbler with just detergent and water, no silver, for a few hours. When I go out of town for a week or so, I transfer the shot from the rubber-lined drum to an earthenware pot, on which is exquisitely depicted a satyr, a nymph, and a centaur.

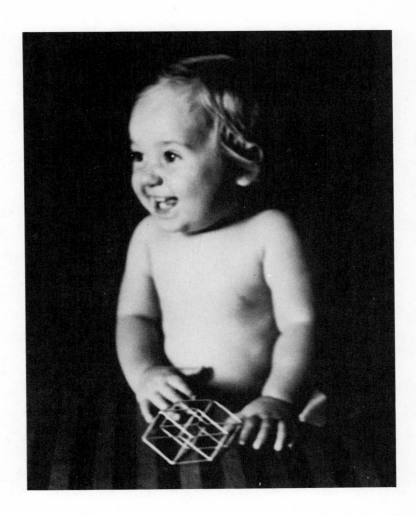

Stones, Rings, and Measurement

pennyweight scale
stone-caliper
ring sizer
ring mandrel
half-round pliers
roundnose pliers
ring clamp
equalling file
hand drill
round wire drawplate for 20 gauge and finer
round wire drawplate for 12 gauge to 20 gauge
(optional)
square wire drawplate for 12 gauge to 20 gauge
(optional)
drawtongs (optional)
oval and round bracelet mandrels (optional)

Precious metals are weighed in the troy system. The troy ounce is roughly 1.1 avoirdupois ounces, the common everyday ounce. Twelve troy ounces make a troy pound; the ounce is subdivided into twenty pennyweights (abbreviated *dwt.*), and each pennyweight into twenty-four grains. The troy ounce is equal to a little over thirty-one grams metric.

The metric system crops up in measuring stones, too. Cabochons and other gemstone shapes are measured in millimeters — a single figure for a round stone (2 mm.) and two for the short and long axes of ovals (8 mm. x 10 mm.). Setting a stone with smaller dimensions than 6 mm. may be difficult, with more and more of the stone disappearing into the setting; on the other hand, stones with longer dimensions than 18 mm. or so will probably be suitable only for a large bracelet or a pendant. Anything smaller will do for a ring.

Stones are weighed in karats; the metric karat is one-fifth of a gram, or a little over three grains troy. The height of a cabochon can vary wildly: moonstones are often cut as high as they are broad at the base in order to exploit their refractive quality, so that an 8 mm. moonstone is likely to be a great deal higher than an 8 mm. agate. Moreover, since different minerals have different densities, size is no guide to weight unless you know the specific gravity of the mineral in front of you. Chrysocola, or Eilat-stone (a copper ore) is a third as heavy as agate (silica). The dimensions of a particular stone can be easily verified, though: a good pocket stone-caliper, with inches on one side and millimeters on the other, is available from jewelers' suppliers for about five dollars.

The thickness of silver wire or sheet is measured with a wire gauge; this has a series of holes graduated in B&S gauge numbers on one side (4 gauge to 36 gauge, the numbers going up as the thickness goes down). Decimal equivalents are given on the other side of the gauge; thus 14 gauge equals .064 inches, 18 gauge equals .040 inches, etc. B&S gauge is nonlinear, as a comparison of the decimal equivalents rapidly reveals; nevertheless, it's here to stay as far as the jewelry trades are concerned and one gets used to it after a while.

Hardness is usually measured on the Mohs scale, where certain common stones of various hardnesses are assigned even numbers. Thus talc is Mohs 1 hardness, gypsum 2, all the way up to sapphire (hardness 9) and diamond (hardness 10), in Dr. Mohs's time the hardest thing there was. (Since then harder substances have been synthesized.) The Mohs scale is nonlinear, too, but the important thing to know is what will scratch what, and act accordingly. For example, your steel pliers will not scratch agate (Mohs 7 or 8) but will scratch silver (Mohs 2.5 or so) and malachite (Mohs 4), another copper ore. Do not confuse hardness with brittleness, however: moonstone is hard but easily shattered if struck sharply. Opals, on the other hand, are not only soft but brittle as well, and consequently must not only be set carefully, but also set in such a way that the stone will be protected from chance concussions.

Ring sizes are linear but seemingly arbitrary. The tapered steel ring mandrel is marked off in quarter sizes from size 1 to size 13. The ring sizer is a series of graduated rings, sized one to thirteen by half sizes, corresponding to the sizes on the mandrel. To make a ring size 4 requires a strip of metal 50 mm. long; for size 5, use a strip 52½ mm. long; and so on up (or down). One size on the mandrel is equal to a quarter

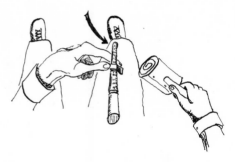

Bending ring blank over mandrel with mallet

centimeter of the length of the band for the ring. Usually you will want to estimate low, by a size or even two, in order to allow for the ring's stretching when you form or planish it; that way, it will come out about right. Another reason for underestimating is that when it comes time to fit a ring to its wearer, it is a lot less work to stretch a ring up a half-size than to cut it down once it is stretched too far.

To make a quarter-inch band ring, start with a strip of flat stock, which comes in ⅛-, ¼-, and ⅜-inch widths, among others. Cut the flat strip to the proper length, allowing for stretching a size in the planishing. Bend the strip around the mandrel, forming the ends in toward each other with a rawhide mallet. A half-round pliers helps here, since the final alignment of the two sides of what will be the joint may be difficult to do precisely with the mallet and mandrel alone. Having aligned the joint, file it with an equalling file — you will probably want to set the ring in a vise or ring clamp while you do this. Since the cutting faces of the equalling file are parallel, the joint will line up nicely once it is properly filed, and be almost invisible after soldering.

Ring clamp

Equalling file

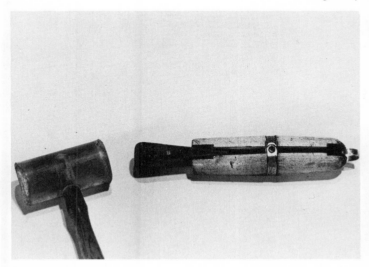

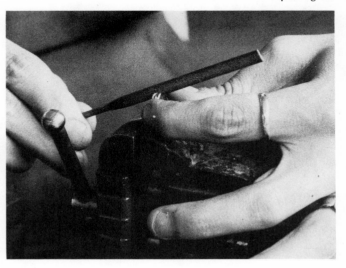

Once you have realigned the joint with pliers (the file will have spread it apart by at least its own width), spray the ring thoroughly with flux as you heat it, and solder the joint. I lay rings on their sides and flow the solder in at the top, allowing gravity to help the solder flow down to the other edge via the joint. After pickling, form the ring round with a mallet, since it will be slightly squashed from aligning the joint with pliers. Then planish the ring and stretch it to the desired size, reversing the ring on the mandrel every so often so the inside will not be tapered. File the rim of the ring both inside and out, so that there will be no sharp edges. Buff the rim with tripoli (which will also grind off any fire-scale resulting from inadequate fluxing); wash the ring in ammonia-water; and polish it with red rouge. This is the basic procedure for making any ring from a strip of silver, whether solid or openwork. Strips for rings can also be made from braided or

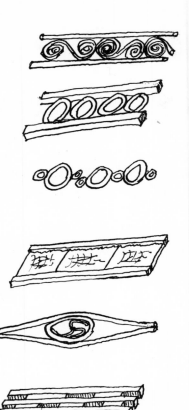

Ring blanks

Braiding wire

twisted wire either plain or with a rim of solid round wire on either side.

To braid wire, first cut three pieces the same length and fix them in a vise side by side. If you are going to braid a long strip (e.g., for a bracelet), clamp the wires at their midpoints, since long strands of wire, over nine inches or so, tend to be a little unmanageable. Holding the center wire in one hand, pull one of the outer wires around the back and twist the two. Then take the other outer wire and the new center wire and twist them the same way, the outer wire always going around the back of the center one. Just keep switching sides, and soon you will have an inch or so of braid. At this point it would be a good idea to slide it down into the vise so that just the two or three twists show, as after an inch or so the braid starts to get loose and it is hard to keep the wire under tension. When you have done one side of a long braided strip, turn it upside down and do the three wires you left dangling free below the vise — being careful not to reverse the braided pattern by clamping it wrong side to.

At the end, square off the whole strip with a rawhide mallet on a surface plate or flat stake. Some silversmiths prefer to solder all three strands separately and consequently leave the squaring-off for last, or even leave the braid loose. Note: a four-strand braid can be made by alternately twisting the inner pair of wires and the two outer pairs.

Twisting wire into long ropes is best done with a hand drill. Cut a long piece of wire about two and a half times the length of the twisted piece you want to end up with. Clamp the two free ends in a vise, and pull the loop tight. Squeeze down the hairpin bend in the middle until the loop will fit into the chuck of your drill, or else clamp the chuck onto a coathook-screw and loop the wire over that. Then, while maintaining a constant tension on the wires, turn the drill. As the wire twists, you will probably have to take a few steps toward the vise. Double-twisted wire may be done the same way: 18 gauge round wire twisted into a double strand combines well with plain 16 gauge round wire for a second twisting. Anneal twisted wire before trying to form it, as the twisting puts a lot of bounce into it and spontaneously uncoils a little when heated.

Rings and bracelets made from twisted or braided wire will take a lot of stretching, easily four sizes; hence it is a good idea to allow for a lot of stretch when estimating the size of the finishing ring, and cut the metal accordingly short. Both twisted and braided work are greatly enhanced by treating with liver-of-sulfur and polishing the high parts.

Bracelets in general are just big rings, with round and oval mandrels of an appropriate size to match. There is no such thing as a bracelet sizer, though, so you are going to have to invent your own measurement system. Mine, for what it's worth, was to scratch lines into the mandrel at one-inch intervals, number them, and make a set of bracelets, one to a size, which double as my sample bangles and are similarly numbered. I have not yet done this for the oval mandrel, partly because a great many oval bracelets are open at the back, so size is less critical.

Drawing wire. Wire finer than 20 gauge may not be readily available from your local jewelers' supplier, or at eleven o'clock in the evening. Furthermore, some silversmiths prefer to draw their 20 gauge solder down a little finer, especially when the work they are soldering is itself as fine as 20 gauge. A steel drawplate has a series of graduated holes through which wire can be pulled successively finer. I own three such plates, one for round wire 12 gauge down to 20 gauge, one for square wire, and a third for round wire 20 gauge down to about 40 gauge, of which the last is by far the most useful. One advantage of the square drawplate, however, is that heavy round wire can be pulled down to medium square. Thus I regularly make 15 gauge square from 12 gauge round.

Since squeezing the wire through the drawplate stresses it, you will have to anneal every five holes or so in a drawing operation. Furthermore, if you are drawing anything heavier than 18 gauge (which can be coiled around itself before an-

Drawing wire through a drawplate

nealing) you may want to consider wrapping the coil of stiff wire in binding wire before you anneal it, or at least wrap some 20 gauge around it at two or three spots. Otherwise, it will uncoil as you heat it, even before you have finished fluxing it.

Solder, on the other hand, need not be annealed. I draw solder by filing the end of a one-ounce coil of it into a point with a long taper. I poke this rat-tail through the widest hole in the drawplate and pull the whole coil through, slowly, using a pair of needle-nose pliers for a drawtong. (For heavier gauges of wire I have a regulation drawtong, whose curved handle makes it easier to get a purchase on while pulling obstinate silver through the plate.) Vise-grip pliers also make good drawtongs. I repeat the process at the next hole, except that if the rat-tail is a little squashed I file it again. Five holes later my solder is 24 gauge and about two and a half times as long as the coil of 20 gauge I started with. This solder is fine enough to solder bezel wire.

Bezels are frames for stones. The usual sort of bezel for a cabochon has a shelf on which the stone sits, with a high wall of flat wire on the outside. Occasionally the shelf may be dispensed with and a flat backing of sheet, soldered to the base of the wall, will support the stone from beneath. In either case the top of the wall is crimped in evenly against the sloping edge of the cabochon; the spring tension imparted to the bezel by smoothing it in around the stone keeps the stone in place, and the metal stays stiff once it has been stressed.

Although flat bezel wire and thin square stock soldered together will make a bezel and a shelf, it is a lot easier to buy bezel wire with the shelf built in. Cross-sections of various types are shown at left. Bezel wire with a low shelf and high wall is particularly handy for moonstones, whose sides are often nearly perpendicular and impossible to hold securely in a bezel with a low wall. On the other hand, high-shelf bezels have plenty of room behind the stone for supports within the bezel, or for filing to fit a band.

Accurate fitting of the bezel to the stone saves a lot of grunting and groaning later, when it comes time to wedge the stone into a bezel that is too small, or get the stone to stop rattling if the bezel is too large. First, round the end of the coil of bezel wire with a half-round pliers, so that the contour of the shelf matches the tightest curve of the stone: this will make it easier to get a purchase later on. Holding the stone in place on the shelf, between your thumb and index finger, with your free hand wrap the bezel wire all the way around the stone, guiding the wire with your thumb and keeping it tight. When you have completely encircled the stone, pinch the bezel as tight as you can hold it, and mark where the joint will come, allowing for a little bit of filing. Snip it off, align the joint, file it with an equalling file, and set it on the soldering pad upside down (that is, shelf-side up), so that when you solder it the solder will not collect on the shelf. Use your finest solder, or a snippet on your soldering probe, since the less solder you can get away with, the less is likely to collect in places you didn't intend it to.

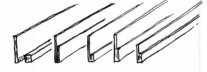

Bezel wire

Before soldering anything else to a bezel, make sure it fits the stone. Like the 18 gauge, ¼-inch ring discussed earlier, a bezel immediately after soldering will be a little squashed and will require some reshaping with half-round pliers before the stone will go into it.

There are several ways to solder a ring band to a bezel. I usually invert the bezel and set the ring on the back, propping it up if necessary with a charcoal block. A ring-soldering stand —a short mandrel of asbestos or high-temperature carbon rod, set in a frame so that the rod is horizontal and elevated about half an inch from the base —makes it possible to solder a ring from any position, and is indispensable for making elaborate settings that have to be constructed right side up. However you position a ring for soldering, remember that the body of the ring is considerably heavier than the bezel, and will need to be heated thoroughly before you try to solder the bezel to it.

Setting the stone can proceed only after soldering is completed, since the heat of soldering will destroy most stones. Pop the stone into the bezel, and smooth the wall around the sides with a burnishing tool or roundnose pliers, being very careful not to scrape the stone itself. This is particularly true of your final pass around the stone, where the setting tool should actually be riding on top of the wall of the bezel,

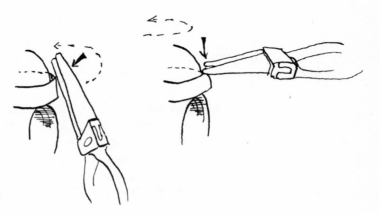

Setting a cabochon with roundnose pliers

stressing it down and into the stone. After the stone is tight, file the marks left on the bezel by the setting tool; then buff the whole bezel with tripoli before polishing the whole ring with jewelers' rouge.

Stones to be hung in earrings will need a jump ring soldered at the top of each bezel. After you have checked the fitting on such bezels, mark the point where you want the jump ring with a stylus, and flow a drop of solder onto where you made the mark. It is a good idea to solder a jump ring on the opposite side of the bezel from the existing joint, to avoid springing the latter open. If you solder your jump ring flat in the same plane as the back of the stone, you will be able to bend the bezel easily at the jump ring when it comes time to set the stone, without having to file any solder away.

In designing jewelry with stones, remember that some stones may need protection from wear or breakage; therefore, avoid setting brittle stones like opals in little-finger rings where they are exposed to a high risk of slamming against something. The wearer's own physical makeup or occupation may affect the design, too: piano players can't play properly while wearing a ring with a wide shank, and active people with short finger joints have problems with wide shanks too. Hence it is a good idea to know some stone settings that are narrow in the shank. One way is to saw wedges out of a plain band, as shown, setting the stone at the widest part. Another method is to solder two or three rings side by side at the back, with steel nails or shims made from broken needle files holding them apart at the front. A third technique is to forge a heavy strip of stock into a U shape, with the ends flared out and rolled if you wish, and the bezel soldered between the two horns.

So far I have discussed rings that are *fabricated,* that is, constructed from wire, flat stock, and so forth. Many rings are cast by the lost-wax process, a method much used by manufacturers desirous of producing multiple castings (not me). In all fairness, lost-wax casting was also used extensively by the great Italian goldsmith Benvenuto Cellini in the 1500s on a

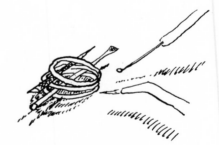

Soldering a three-ring shank

one-shot basis, so it is hardly exclusively a production gimmick. The art in this technique lies not so much in one's competence with metal as the ability to carve a good model in wax, life-size, of the object desired. To this model are attached two sprues of wax rod: these will be the vents in the final mold through which the metal is poured in and the air flowed out.

When the model is finished, it is set in plaster or some other *investment;* when this fireproof jacket has set sufficiently, the wax is burnt out by firing the mold. The two commonest ways of getting the molten metal into the mold are vacuum casting and centrifugal casting; in the first, a pump sucks all the air out of the mold, and the molten metal, when released, fills the vacuum thus created. In the second, a spring-loaded arm, with the mold and crucible on the end, is released to whirl around inside a drum; the hot metal is thrown into the mold by centrifugal force. Both of these methods require expensive equipment; nowadays even fully equipped silversmithing shops often send their waxes out to be cast elsewhere.

chapter
7

Hollowware

Sterling beakers, by T. Brown

Photo: Susan MacDougall

steel-pointed dividers
raising stake
annealing pan and pumice
centerpunch
sandbag
stake extender
bottoming stake
two 16 gauge copper discs, 6-inch diameter
flexible-shaft or hand motor (optional)

I have to confess that when I first decided to learn to raise hollowware I plowed an inordinate amount of money into specialized hammers and stakes, most of which I didn't need then and some of which I have not used to this day. The truth is that you can get by for years with an annealing pan and pumice to fill it, a raising stake, and the forging and crosspeen hammers mentioned in Chapter 4. The raising stake costs about twenty dollars; it fits the socket of your anvil stake. The annealing pan and pumice cost about ten dollars; their use will be described shortly. You will also need a pair of dividers and a centerpunch, and a disc of copper 16 gauge thick and 6 inches across.

Copper is used for practice pieces and prototypes of silver hollowware because the two metals are about equally malleable and copper costs a tenth as much. I say "about equally malleable"; copper when annealed is perceptibly softer than annealed silver, and tends to crack when stiffened sooner than does silver; nevertheless, if you learn to raise copper you will be able to raise silver without much trouble.

Take your copper disc and locate the center. Mark it lightly with a centerpunch, and strike a light line with a stylus from the center to the rim. Then use dividers to mark a series of

will serve to guide your hammer-strokes later, the radius line telling you when you have made one complete course around the outside of the bowl.

Before you begin to work the disc, anneal it. Lay it on the pumice in the annealing pan, and heat it up as you spray flux on one side; when the flux has hardened, turn the disc over with heavy tongs or pliers — anything with which you can get a sure purchase on the hot metal and still not get burnt. Then flux the other side, and continue heating the disc, turning the annealing pan as you do so. This will heat the metal evenly, so that you don't encounter patches of stiff metal when you come to raise it later. Acetylene users please note: your No. 2 tip will not be hot enough to anneal a disc this size. I use a No. 4, and larger discs may require larger tips still.

When the disc glows a dull red in subdued light, turn off the torch and let the metal cool; do not quench it until it has cooled to about 400°F or less, as the metal will cool unevenly, may well warp, and might crack under stress. You may let the disc cool entirely in air, but it will be more difficult to get the flux off than if you quench it from a few hundred degrees; when a drop of water or flux spatters, rather than just dancing around, the disc will be cool enough to quench. Steel-wool *all* remaining flux off before you start to hammer; otherwise the little beads of hard glaze will be driven into the metal and pockmark it, and such pits are very hard to remove later on. On the other hand, if there is fire-scale, you might as well leave it until after the last stroke with the raising hammer, and then buff it off with tripoli before you begin to planish; there is no need to remove fire-scale sooner.

Raising is done by holding the disc at a constant angle to the knob of the raising stake, with the centerpunch mark and circles facing you, and rotating it slowly while striking concentric circles just above the point of contact with the horizontal sharp face of a raising hammer, crosspeen hammer, or forging hammer, starting from the inside and working out. The first circle should be struck while rotating the disc clockwise, following one of the circles; the second, counterclock-

wise, just above the first line and below the second; the third clockwise above the second, on the line above, and so forth out to the edge. Keep the hammer strokes even, and the angle constant throughout each course around the disc. Gradually the side will be stretched up and in, actually thickening the metal towards the rim: hence the term *compressional stretching,* since the metal is actually forced into itself, having nowhere else to go. The sharper the face of the hammer, the more pronounced this one-way stretch will be; providing the silversmith works evenly around the back of a disc, keeping the angle constant, a 6-inch disc can be raised into a jar whose sides are almost perpendicular, whose diameter at the top is considerably less than 6 inches, and whose rim is noticeably thicker than the original disc.

Three problems are likely to arise, however. First, it is hard to gauge the angle of the disc against the stake when you can't actually *see* it. After a while, though, you will learn to guess this by feel; meanwhile, do the best you can. A second problem is that your left hand will probably get very tired. If so, rest between courses; as long as the angle is the same throughout a single course, a slight change when you go back to work can be corrected in a subsequent series of courses. A third problem is that individual bulges may start to appear as you work; these can be corrected locally with the sharp end of the crosspeen hammer, and indeed such hammers are ideal for just this sort of spot-work, and are sometimes called *spotting hammers* instead.

Once you have done your first series of courses out to the rim, and corrected any chance bulges on the side, you will be left with a flaring bowl whose bottom may already be close to the shape you ultimately want, but whose sides will want to be stretched in quite a bit still. Anneal the bowl — flux the inside first, then the outside — and start your inside course just where the sides diverge from your intended shape, again stretching the metal over the curve of the stake by striking just above the point of contact of the inside of the bowl with the stake. If a second series of courses doesn't do it, go for a third; as long as you anneal the metal evenly on the annealing pan when it stiffens up, you can count on being able to stretch the sides of the bowl up almost vertically, should your design call for it. After your last raising course, buff off any fire-scale that has collected during annealing; there is no need to anneal the metal before planishing it.

Planish the metal in alternating clockwise and counterclockwise circles from the center of the bowl out, much as you worked it with the raising hammer, with this difference: whereas you struck the metal just *above* the point of contact with the stake when *raising* it, you will want to *planish* the bowl with the stake directly *underneath* the bowl where the hammer hits it. Start with a hammer whose face is comparatively convex, since you will first of all want to obliterate the wedge-shaped marks left by the raising hammer. After the first series of courses, planish the bowl again with a hammer of less convexity, and again with the flat-faced side of your planishing hammer at last. (Since both bowl and stake are convex, as long as your aim is good you will run little risk of denting the surface with the abrupt edge of the flat face.)

You may also wish to thicken the edge of the bowl between planishing courses. Holding the bowl on your lap or on a sandbag, strike down the high spots on the rim with the planishing or spotting hammer, hardening the metal just below the rim with an additional planishing course after you have done a full course in the rim itself. Repeating this process six or eight times will accentuate the thickness of a rim already thickened by compressional stretching, making it very strong. This process is called *caulking* by silversmiths, and is first cousin to the *upsetting* practiced extensively by blacksmiths (as in forging nail-heads).

On the other hand, you may wish only to file the rim flat, or, alternately, to beat it very thin, accentuating a flaring edge. Another possibility is to solder an ornamental band of silver to the rim at the top; flat-backed beaded wire, for example, has been used for this purpose in Philadelphia ever since the late eighteenth century. It is all a matter of taste.

Five rim cross-sections: (left to right) filed even, caulked, flared, with molding added, flattened

Planishing the bowl: outside . . .

. . . and inside

Copper switchplate and bowl, by T. Brown

A third possibility is to restore the rim to a horizontal plane, like the top of a baptismal basin. The trick to this is not to raise or planish the metal all the way to the rim, but to straighten out the rim itself by striking it with a rawhide mallet against the top of a block of wood held in a vise. Two nails driven into the block will serve as a guide so that the edge of the rim will always be a constant distance in from the edge of the block underneath as you rotate the piece of hollowware; once the rim is formed flat, planish it on both sides, with the flat center of your anvil stake or a surface plate underneath.

You will have little trouble buffing and polishing the outside of a bowl or other piece of hollowware; the inside, however, may be inaccessible to your buffing wheel. The best solution by *hand* is steel wool, followed by sandpaper, followed by finer sandpaper. This does not leave a high polish, to be sure, but the matte surface it *does* leave will be as even as you can scour and will contrast pleasantly with the shine of the outside surface. (You may also smooth the surface by hand with a well-oiled burnishing tool.) On the other hand, there *are* polishing motors that will enable you to get in there, notably the hand motor and the flexible shaft.

Hand motors are relatively cheap; the Dremel Moto-tool is about twenty-five dollars and I know at least one maker of miniature sailboats who has used hers for a number of years and swears by it. The hand motor terminates in a small drill-chuck, which will hold drills, arbors for wire and abrasive wheels and small circular saws, stone-setting and cutting burrs, and many other types of bits. The flexible-shaft motor also terminates in a chuck, but the handpiece is on the end of a shaft which is driven by a motor hung up on the wall, and controlled by a foot-rheostat. Although a new flexible-shaft motor and footswitch, complete, costs about a hundred dollars, a satisfactory one can be constructed from a sewing machine motor and a separate handpiece and shaft, the latter set available from any large hardware store for about twenty-five dollars. Tom Brown's flexible shaft is a hybrid of this sort and works quite well. Occasionally, used dental engines come up for sale, often at a considerable saving.

Suppose you want a bowl with a flat bottom. For this you will need a small, round, flat-topped bottoming stake and an extension stake-holder, about five dollars each. The latter fits into your anvil stake-holder; the socket at the top will fit a number of small stakes — round, flat rectangular, Hardie (wedge-shaped), and others. The extension holder lifts the stake high above the stake-holder and stump, so that you can easily get at the work from all sides.

When you want to flatten the bottom of a bowl, set it upside down on the bottoming stake and strike it with a mallet, being careful to keep the bowl centered (your concentric circles and centerpunch mark should help you here). When you are done, the bottom of the bowl will be flat and the sides will have a little ridge along the bottom; planish this area stiff. For additional strength, the bottom may be domed up into the bowl with a planishing hammer over a sandbag, tapping lightly in a spiral from the center out.

Now that you have raised a 6-inch disc, you will find that 4-inch discs will do nicely for smaller vessels, and, moreover, take a great deal less time. A 4-inch disc has less than half the metal of a 6-inch one, given that the two are of equal

Bottoming stake and extender

thickness; hence a silver disc 4 inches across is only about fifteen dollars, and well within the range of the small shop's resources. Make sure you have raised enough copper that you know what you are doing; and at least for your maiden piece of silver hollowware, do one to exactly the same design in copper first.

Another method of making hollowware is *dropping* or *hollowing*. Hollowing is stretching a piece of metal into a depression by working the *inside* with round-faced mallets and hammers; we have already encountered hollowing into lead in the making of the bowl of the spoon in Chapter 4. Other variants are *repoussé*, in which the metal is struck with hammers or punches against a backstop of pitch, and *dapping*, where the metal is struck into a hemispherical depression in a block of wood or steel with a steel punch, the block having several different sizes of pockets with a punch to match each. Hollowing a disc of metal into a bowl can also be done on a sandbag, but the usual procedure is to carve a depression the size and shape of the desired bowl and hollow the disc into that, covering the trough with a sheet of leather or suede to prevent wood-grain, cracks, or chisel marks from scarring the outside of the bowl.

Discs for hollowing should be centerpunched and marked with circles as before, but this time the circles go on the inside. Begin by tipping the rim into your depression, and striking just inside it with a round-faced hammer. Do the second course just inside the first, and so forth in to the center, the reverse of your raising procedure. The sides will pull in a little as you do this, but by no means as much as they would had you chosen to raise the same disc into the same shape; meanwhile the metal of the sides will be stretched *down* and *out* (tensional stretching) as opposed to the *up* and *in* (compressional stretching) of raising. When you first start to work, you will be striking the metal down into an air space created by the difference in curvature of your bowl and the mold; when planishing later on, make sure that the bowl and

Pewtersmith Chris March

106

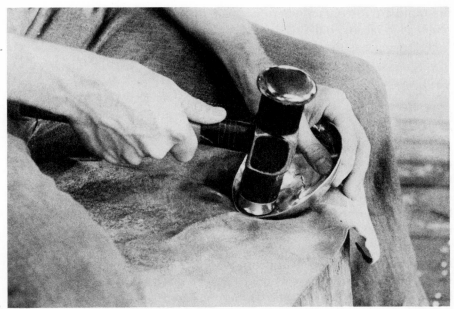

Hollowing bowl into stump
Mold for hollowing pewter

the mold are in contact where you are about to strike them, much as in raising, only inside out.

Hollowing has the advantage that you can stretch a great deal of metal with relatively little effort; hence it is a favored technique for summer camps (where, also, many people will use the same mold). For a single piece, however, it is silly to go to the trouble of chiseling out a depression, when the whole job could be done a lot quicker with a raising hammer and stake. Moreover, hollowing is only good for making objects whose sides are perpendicular or less; it is useless, as hollower Chris Murch pointed out, to form a piece of metal on a mold from which it cannot be extricated. On the other hand, it is the only reasonable way to make a run of four or more identical pieces of hollowware with a hammer.

Another method widely used to make hollowware, both in silver and pewter, is to spin it on a lathe, forcing the metal sideways against a convex wooden or steel mold by pressing hard against it with a wooden burnisher. Few silversmiths in the eighteenth century had a lathe, however, and those few that did often advertised themselves as turners first and metal-smiths second (see, for example, the Philadelphia turner's ad reproduced on p. 122 of Kauffman's *The Colonial Silversmith*).

It is fairly simple to construct hollowware out of sheet; this technique became common in colonial America during the life of Paul Revere, and indeed he made a number of objects by this method rather than the traditional raising from a disc. It is significant that in the Copley portrait of Revere the silver-smith is shown contemplating a spherical teapot, not a straight-sided one, as though to document the fact that he knew very well how to raise silver from discs with a hammer. Nevertheless, once the rolling mill became available in the colonies — on much the same terms as the lathe, not every shop having one — it was no longer necessary to raise up the sides of beakers, tankards, cans, and other straight-sided vessels when the same result could be had with less time and skill by wire-binding silver sheet together, soldering the joints, and planishing the results. In a coffeepot the handle would be soldered on over the seam up the side, partially concealing it; and for those homesick for the thick rims of raised hollowware a decorative band could be soldered on at the top. The cigarette humidor designed by Tom Brown, shown in exploded view, was designed to be constructed by this method — which, of the methods described above, is the *only* way to produce hollowware that *could* be illustrated with an exploded drawing.

Rendering of Tom Brown's cigarette humidor, drawn by Tom Brown

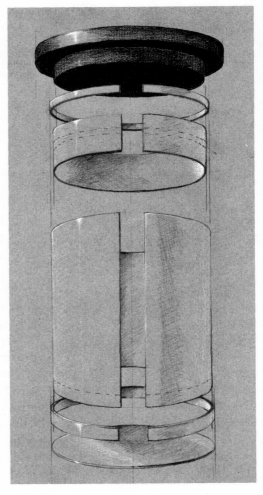

Exploded drawing of same piece, drawn by Tom Brown

Sterling beaker, by T. Brown

In fairness to myself I must admit that although most of the hammers and stakes I bought back when I began to do raising proved superfluous at first, a lot of them came in handy later, and I have had the additional satisfaction of having bought them when they were cheap, instead of waiting until I needed them and the price had gone up. Here are the ones I have found most useful:

— *The crimping stake,* or *valley stake* crimps the sides of a large disc in toward the center, by creasing it into the valleys with a raising hammer *along* the radii, which makes subsequent raising go a lot quicker.

— *The cowhorn stake* enables you to have a surface to work against for deep objects with narrow necks. Both this and the crimping stake fit the anvil stake-holder.

— *The 2-inch stake-holder* has a hole at the back suitable for a ½-inch bolt or screw, and holds the two stakes which follow. It should be mounted so that its square socket overhangs the edge of your stump or worktable, like the smaller stake-holder.

— *The mushroom stake,* a hemisphere of cast-iron, is good for forming or planishing medium-sized bowls.

— *The large bottoming stake* has a flat top which is good for planishing the rims of basins and other flat pieces (flatware before it is bent, for example). Both it and the mushroom stake are *very* susceptible to rust and pitting, so do not succumb to the temptation to press them into daily service in place of the middle section of your anvil stake, which is both harder and more rust-resistant.

— The *deep planishing hammer* has extra-long faces — 2½ inches from the center of the handle — suitable for planishing the insides of deep bowls.

— The *hollowing hammer* is essentially a forging hammer with curved, rounded faces for working inside; in a pinch it can double as a heavy raising hammer.

More hammers: (left to right) hollowing, repoussé, forging, raising, and chasing (with chasing punches)

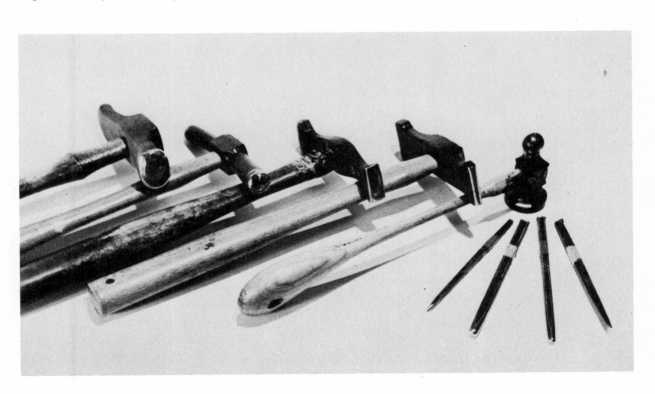

— The *snarling iron* is neither hammer nor stake, but a little of both. It is a bar of flexible steel whose smaller end terminates in a polished knob, bent up at a right angle, and whose other end is bent the opposite way and clamped in a vise. Like the cowhorn stake, it is meant to get inside deep vessels; but in this case the punch is from *within*: the pot is set on the ball end and the bar struck with a mallet. The ball strikes the inside of the pot on the rebound, bulging it out. Revere undoubtedly used a snarling iron in the manufacture of the globular teapot mentioned above.

A final word should be said about raising and forming tools in related fields: if you don't find the hammer you want at the jewelers' supplier, check out the section in the hardware stores for automobile bodywork. After all, car fenders are hollowware too.

Copper bowl and ashtray, by N. Humez

chapter

8

Surface
Textures

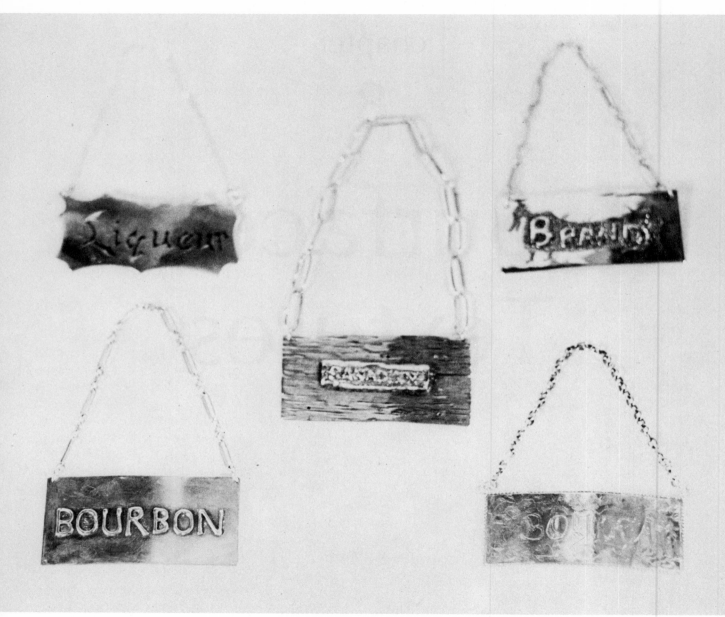

graph paper
binding wire
pitchbowl and pitch
chasing hammer
chasing punches
graver
repoussé hammer (optional)

In previous chapters I have discussed planishing, burnishing, casting in charcoal, and fusing — all ways of imparting texture to a metal surface prior to finishing. Piercing alters the texture, too, in a negative way: it is the removal of some of the metal by drilling and sawing to create a lattice or other open design. This technique is used extensively by silversmiths Douglas French and Michael Moore of Burlington, Vermont.

A pierced design is a little like a design for a stencil: all center pieces must be attached to the sides (no 0's or figure 8's). For an intricate design it is a good idea to draw the pattern to size on a piece of graph paper, which you then paste onto the silver sheet for the actual drilling and sawing. A plainer pattern may be penciled directly on the metal and painted over with nail polish to protect it from smudging; when all the drilling and sawing is done, the nail polish can be burnt off or dissolved in hot pickle, and the remainder rubbed off with an eraser.

Strike the metal with a centerpunch at every place where you will want to turn the saw abruptly, or just take a breather — at either end of a curved line, or at corners. Drill holes where you have centerpunched the metal, and insert a sawblade through one of the holes before clamping the blade in the frame. (For the proper insertion of sawblades in a frame,

see Chapter 2.) I generally clamp the silver sheet in a vise, and work the saw horizontally; Doug French prefers to hold the silver in one hand, or in a ring clamp, in order to saw vertically. Whichever you choose, keep the sawblade perpendicular to the sheet of silver, *not* angled into the work as would be the case with a wood saw.

It is a good idea to have two thicknesses of sawblade — say, 00 and 1 — and to use the finer blade for sawing the design out. Saw out subsidiary patterns first, leaving the connecting of the lines for last; this way, you will preserve the structural strength of the metal until the last few cuts, which would tend to pull the metal askew were they sawed pre-

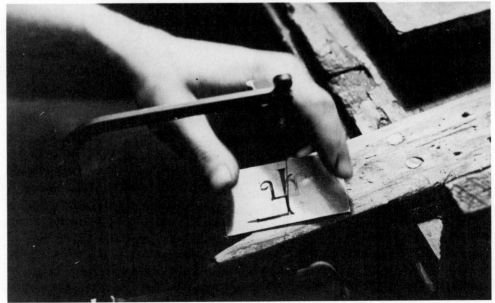

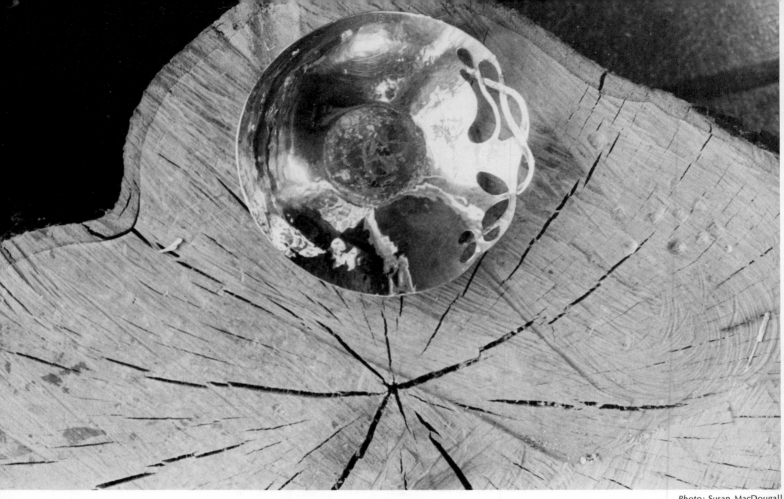

Bowl with pierced rim, by T. Brown

Photo: Susan MacDougall

maturely. Once all the lines have been cut, you can go over some of the lines with the heavier sawblade, which evens out some of the wiggles in the earlier sawing. On the other hand, you may wish to saw out a simple pattern of bold lines with the thicker blade to begin with, and use a finer blade later as a kind of equalling file that can go around corners. Any remaining burrs from sawing may be removed from the edge of the cut with a riffle file.

If you have cut your design into heavy sheet — the handle of a porridge bowl, for example, traditionally an openwork design — you may leave your finishing to be done until after the rest of the piece is completed and ready for finishing also. French and Moore, however, use thin pierced sheet silver in combination with a solid backing. For this method you will want another piece of sheet silver, slightly larger than the pierced one, in readiness for soldering. First, however, you will want to polish both sides of the pierced top layer, eliminating all burrs: if you don't get them now, they will be impossible to remove once the pierced and solid sheets of silver are soldered together.

Mix up a small quantity of yellow ochre. French and Moore keep handy a jar lid with a small quantity of yellow ochre in it to which they add a little bit of water whenever they need to contain solder flow; after tying the pierced and solid pieces together with binding wire they paint the design itself with ochre and the edge of the two plates with flux. (Remember to keep flux and ochre from touching each other!) Both flux and

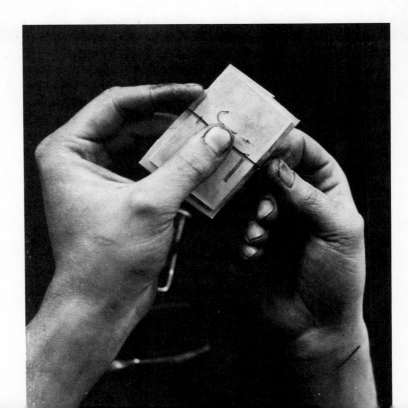

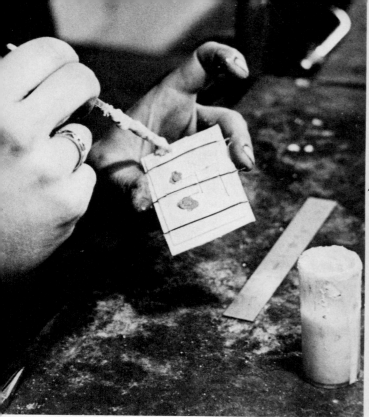
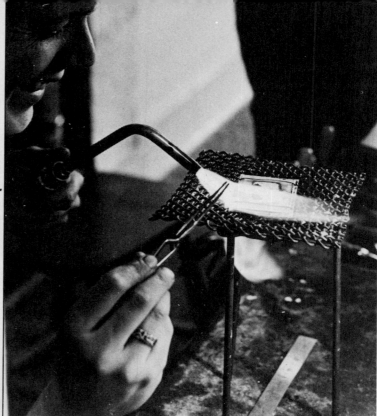

ochre should be allowed to dry thoroughly before soldering commences.

When soldering two-layered pierced work, French and Moore make use of a soldering tripod with a screen on top to hold the work so that it can be heated evenly from below. When the silver is hot enough, the solder is flowed in at the sides of the work, just enough to make a good seam, and no more. Once the solder has been applied to all four sides of the work, the binding wire is cut off and the work quenched in pickle. The edges are then sawed off even and filed. The pierced piece is then ready to be incorporated into the larger design — in the case of a small pendant, this means merely soldering a jump ring on at top center — and the whole treated with liver-of-sulfur, buffed, and polished.

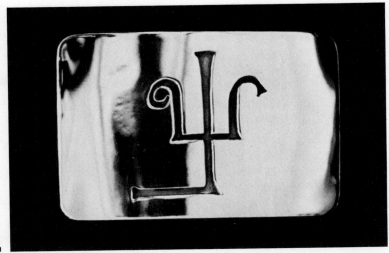

Pierced buckle, by D. French

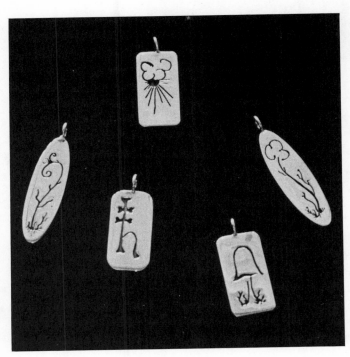

Pierced pendants, by D. French and M. Moore

Pierced rings, by D. French and M. Moore

The same method may be used to make rings; here, however, you must be careful when bending the soldered work that the top sheet doesn't bend out and away at the center; tap it carefully back into place with a mallet as soon as it starts to do so. For best results, a pierced design for a ring should be confined mostly to the center of the ring blank, and not wander too far over towards the edge; otherwise you run the risk of the joint splitting under the stresses of forming the ring — and such delamination is a great bother to repair later. If you confine your piercing to the middle of the top band, you will avoid this problem entirely.

Repoussé, and its half-sibling *chasing,* are methods of hollowing; they are used to create a pattern in relief on a limited area of metal without altering the shape of the piece as a

Chasing into pitchbowl

whole. At times repoussé and hollowing really overlap, as when the side of a teapot immediately beneath the intended location of the spout is formed out with a small-faced repoussé hammer against a sandbag; smaller areas, however, are more usually worked against a lead block or pitch in a pitchbowl, with a chasing hammer and punches rather than a hammer alone. Both pitchbowl and pitch are available from your jewelers' supplier; to get the pitch into the pitchbowl, heat the entire can (after you have loosened the lid) in a saucepan of water until the pitch is ready to flow; then pour it from the can into the iron bowl, where it will solidify as it cools. To immobilize a piece of flat silver in the pitch prior to doing repoussé, bend the corners down slightly and heat the silver with your torch until it sinks into the pitch — being *very* careful not to ignite the pitch itself! When the pitch has set, rough out the design with your chasing tools and hammer, working from the edges into the center, and being careful not to try to stretch the metal too much at first: like hollowing, repoussé stretches the metal a lot in the middle and very little on the sides. Working from the outside in tends to shove the metal inward, thickening it up again in the very places it tends to be stretched thinnest.

Note that chasing hammers have very broad heads and thin, springy handles. The broad face is so that you don't have to watch where the hammer hits and can concentrate your attention on the lower end of the chasing tool instead. The springy handle is so that the hammer-blow will be percussive without the need for a broad swing under brute force: it is, after all, the chasing punch, not the hammer, that is doing the work.

Since the pitch is still slightly flexible at room temperature, striking the metal against it with punches shoves the work into the pitch, much as lead yields when silver is hollowed into it. Hence when you wish to remove the work to anneal it or turn it over, you will have to heat the silver before the pitch behind it softens sufficiently for the work to be pried loose. Any pitch adhering to the metal can be burnt off when you anneal the work — and you should do so every time you turn it over to work the other side.

Suppose you are doing a bunch of grapes. Presumably you will have formed the grapes with a round punch and the stem with a wedge-shaped one. Now when you turn the work over, you will probably want to deepen the grooves between the grapes with a wedge-shaped tool; in addition, the stem may be accentuated by chasing a groove on either side. If the detail is not pronounced enough, flop the work again, work the back, and repeat until you have gotten the desired degree of relief.

Chasing on the outside of a pot is done by filling the vessel itself with pitch and chasing in against that; after the outside has been worked the whole pot is heated up and the pitch poured out.

Tom Brown driving punch

Punch and punched sterling discs, by T. Brown

Some silversmiths texture the surface of metal with punches having patterns cut into the face of the tool, a mirror image of which will be produced on the metal with a single blow of the chasing hammer. The extensive use of this method by Indian silversmiths in the American Southwest is said to have originated in the highly decorative punch-work characteristic of Spanish and Mexican leather craftsmen. Many traditional designs are available from Rio Grande Jewelers' Supply; alternately, you can make your own from tool steel, or send away to Allcraft for a design made to order. (See sources of supply, p. 177.)

In this same category fall standard marks — *sterling, 14 K,* and the like — and maker's marks, the use of which is regulated both by industry and by law. Maker's marks are a form of trademark and must be registered as such. See "Understanding the National Stamping Act" in *American Jewelry Manufacturer,* Nov., 1970, by Joel A. Windman, Counsel to the Jewelers Vigilance Committee, 919 Third Ave., N.Y., N.Y. 10022.

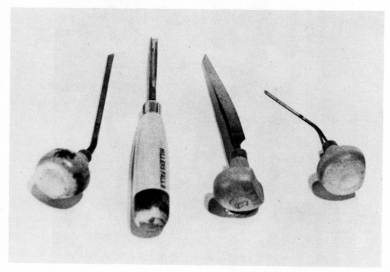

Gravers

Metal can be textured with a graver, using the pitchbowl to hold the work firm as you did for repoussé. Gravers are held with the ball of the handle against the ball of your thumb, with your thumb running the length of the shaft and steadying it. Ideally gravers should be sawed off and reground so that the tip of the graver is less than a quarter-inch beyond the end of your thumb; gravers are usually sold way too long in the expectation that you will cut them down to your own size. When you want to engrave a design, it helps to scratch it onto the metal with a steel stylus first, and use the graver to deepen the lines, rather than trying to plow into the metal with no guide at all, although presumably an experienced hand-engraver — of whom there are pitifully few left alive and working, and those mostly in their advancing years — could probably execute a design freehand without scratching out guidelines first.

A shellac stick, first cousin to the lapidary's dop stick, can substitute for the pitchbowl or graver's block for a very small piece of work. On the other hand, large plates need no vise at all, and hollowware can be rested on a sandbag alone. Plate-engraving was a profitable part of Paul Revere's work, his most famous piece being the Boston Massacre broadside of 1770.

First cousin to the graver is the *florentining* tool, a graver with multiple points used to scratch parallel lines at a single stroke. The florentining tool is usually used in a crisscross pattern to form a meshlike appearance.

Bright-cutting is striking the metal with a sharp little chisel, the blade of the tool burnishing the metal as it cuts. This method is used a great deal by metalsmiths of the Far East — I have a pair of silver chopsticks with bright-cutting, sent me as a child by an uncle stationed in Korea, and I have seen exquisitely chiseled hollowware from Thailand since — but has yet, so far as I know, to be extensively employed in this country.

Etching is selective removal of metal by dissolving it in acid, and is a hazardous procedure; I mention it here more for your information than from any recommendation that you go out and try it. Briefly stated, etching requires that the metal be coated with a substance impervious to acid, called a *resist;* this is usually an asphaltum-based compound which is soluble in turpentine. The *mordant* (literally, "biting agent") is usually nitric acid, mixed one part stock solution to two parts water — with the acid poured into the water, never the other way around; veterans of any chemistry course will tell you how it fizzes and spatters you if you add the water to the acid. Stock nitric acid will eat skin tissues away. With diluted acid you will have a few seconds after contamination in which to flood the acid off your skin with running water, but the most serious drawback, according to Tom Brown, is that you don't *feel* anything until the damage is already done. Consequently, jewelers' supply houses usually carry a less dangerous mordant than nitric acid for general precious metal use; but it is a far weaker mordant and does not do the job on the metal anywhere near as well.

The mordant should be kept in a glass dish or tank deep enough to submerge your piece to be etched entirely. The work should be manipulated with wooden or plastic tongs — this as much to avoid scratching through the resist as to avoid the tongs themselves dissolving in the mordant. When you have scratched your design through the resist down to the bare metal, immerse the work in the mordant, agitating it in the acid to shake off any bubbles which form at the scratches, since the bubbles interfere with the chemical reaction and will make for an unevenly etched line. Half an hour in 1:2 nitric acid should do the trick; any longer and you may well have undercutting in the cracks, where the mordant actually eats under the resist, leaving a shelf. Check the work frequently, as differences in temperature will alter the speed of the chemical reaction.

Three stages of etching: (left to right) before emersion in mordant, during etching, excessive etching causing undercutting

Once the work is done, store or dispose of the nitric acid solution safely — remember that it eats copper plumbing — and thoroughly wash all vessels, countertops, tongs, etc., that have been in contact with the acid, including, of course, the metal you have etched. Remove the resist with turpentine, disposing of the rags or paper towels you have used so that they will not start a fire by spontaneous combustion later on.

A variation of the above is *photo-etching;* here the resist is light-sensitive, so that patches of it will dissolve in the development process depending on whether they have been exposed or not. This technique is used primarily in the manufacture of printed circuits; but I have seen it done to good effect with a photograph on flat silver. Nor should this surprise anyone, since the earliest photographic experiments were on plates coated with silver nitrate, and silver bromide to this day is the major light-sensitive ingredient of photographic emulsions.

Daguerrotypy

chapter
9
Fasteners, Hinges, and Boxes

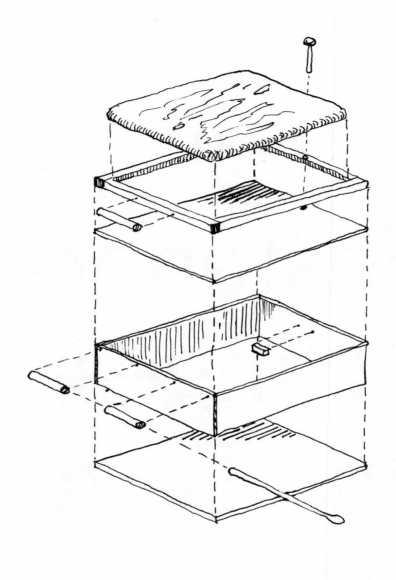

riveting tool
3-inch 16 gauge inside diameter tubing, sterling
3-inch 18 gauge inside diameter tubing, sterling
3-inch 20 gauge inside diameter tubing, sterling

Spring ring

The simplest fastener is the split jump ring alluded to in Chapter 2. A jump ring is a circle of round wire, usually 20 gauge or finer, whose joint has been equaled but is left unsoldered. The silver in commercial jump rings is usually stress-hardened to begin with, so that after being opened and closed into position such jump rings are thoroughly stiff, and will bear a surprising amount of pulling before they stretch open. Still, it is better to solder the jump ring closed if you can, using the snippet-and-probe method, since any jump ring will give way if yanked hard enough and, as we all know, a chain is only as strong as that weakest link. There are two situations in which you will *not* want to solder the jump ring closed: (1) when you can't do so without melting the surrounding metal or annealing the spring of a spring ring (see below); (2) when you *want* the jump ring to give way when yanked (as an alternative to the wearer being choked by a chain).

Spring rings are hollow tubular rings of silver containing a spring and a tiny bolt; the bolt slides across an opening in the side of the spring ring when retracted against the spring, and snaps back across the opening into the tubing on the other side when released. Spring rings can bear more stress than an unsoldered jump ring, but will still pull asunder if tugged hard. Spring rings usually have a small jump ring soldered onto the back; I prefer the type that is already soldered closed, since it is virtually impossible to apply heat to any part of a spring ring without annealing the spring.

Other types of fasteners rely on the force of gravity on the pieces they connect, or on the forces being in the opposite direction from the way the catch must move to be opened. A simple hook for a chain necklace can be made by fusing the end of a stick of round wire the same gauge as that used for the necklace. Solder the unbeaded end of the stick to the last link in the chain; then bend it into a hook so that the opening between the ball and shaft of the hook is just wide enough to allow a link of the neckchain to slip through. When you have formed the hook, planish it stiff. (The same hook clasp will work on a bracelet, but the hook on a bracelet must be bent in such a way that the bracelet cannot be removed except by design, whereas with a necklace the fact that the silver hangs down from the clasp over the neck suffices to keep the hook in place.)

A commercial adaptation of this idea is the sister hook, which consists of two hooks facing in opposite directions and swiveling on a rivet; the insides of the hooks are flat so that they turn flush with each other, with considerable overlap when the sister hook is closed. Both sister hooks and spring rings are used as safety clasps; such clasps are made to augment the main fastener of heavy bracelets or wristwatches, by connecting the two sides with a length of chain that will hold the piece on the wrist loosely when the main catch is opened.

Since silver can be work-hardened, its own springiness may be exploited to make a fastener. *Tie bar* stock is sold hard-rolled to begin with, and needs only to be bent back against itself to form a clip that will hold tie to shirt. *Hair clips* usually consist of a main piece, in its simplest form a convex shell with a hole on either end, and a straight, stiff post, which goes through both holes. The shell can be either openwork or solid; but in either case both post and shell must be forged and planished stiff in order that the spring of the metal will

Sister hooks

Forged hair clip

hold the hair captive. If you make a hair clip by drilling holes in sheet stock, use a larger bit for one hole than for the other, and forge both ends of the post after threading it through the hole so that it will not pass through the smaller hole, thus preventing the loss of the post (a common problem with hair clips). Some hairpieces have comb teeth soldered on as well, which undoubtedly improves the grip.

Riveting will join two pieces together without soldering; multiple rivets will immobilize the two pieces to be joined, but a single rivet will allow them to pivot against each other (as in the sister hook discussed above). Hence riveting is a good way of connecting small parts in a miniature working model, such as the steering device of the Royal Salvo Tricycle shown in the accompanying illustration, where back-and-

Detail from "Royal Salvo Tricycle," by N. Humez

forth motion is to be converted to circular motion or vice versa.

If you have only one rivet, the holes in the two pieces which the rivet is to connect need not be drilled simultaneously, since there will be no problem of alignment. When two or more rivets are to be used, however, you should drill both pieces at once, clamping them in a vise or ring clamp. Drill your first hole, using a bit for which you have matching-diameter wire, as a No. 65 bit and 20 gauge wire. Cut a short piece of that wire a little longer than the total thickness of the two pieces to be riveted, insert it into the hole, and flatten out first one side and then the other over the edge of the hole, tapping it out with the ball end of a ball peen hammer. Drill for the next rivet only after the first is set, for best alignment.

When joining thick pieces of metal you may want to countersink the outside of the rivet hole on both sides; this enables you to have rivets spread out at the heads but still flush with the surface of the metal. Another trick with countersunk holes is to bead one end of the rivet by fusing; insert the rivet, spread out the narrow end of the rivet with a hammer, and then file both sides. Rivet heads may be finished off by striking them with a riveting tool, a steel rod with a concave tip, rather like a carpenter's nail set. If you want the rivets to stand out, you may wish to try making them of a different metal than the pieces joined: copper or yellow gold will contrast nicely with silver. If you use large rivets, you make the spreading of the heads easier by filing a notch in the ends; sawing a groove down the middle will make it possible to bend the ends back and still make it possible to remove the rivet later (for parts of a model that are to be taken off for cleaning, for example). Rivets can also be made of silver tubing; the ends are flared out over the edge of the rivet hole with a burnisher, leaving a hollow center suitable for holding a shaft that must turn.

Hinges are made from tubing sawed into three (or more) sections, the outer sections soldered to the lid and the inner section to the box, tankard, or whatever the lid is to cover.

Alignment is critical: not only must the tubing be soldered in such a way that a pin (of the same diameter as the inside diameter of the tube) will pass through all sections freely, but also the sections themselves must fit side-by-side with no gaps or the hinge will be wobbly. Marking the position of the center section on the lid with a stylus is essential to proper alignment. I often line up the two outer sections of tubing by soldering them with a pin actually in them (being careful not to solder the pin to the tubing). I also place the outer sections of tubing a little closer together than the center section is long; after soldering the center section to the lid, I file it down on either end so that it fits properly between the two outer sections. So that setting the hinge pin does not knock the hinge out of alignment, I bead one end of the pin by fusing, and file a notch in the other to minimize the force needed to set the pin in firmly.

Hinges on tankard lids often have two pieces of tubing, sliced lengthwise, mounted on the center section and outer sections respectively so that when the lid opens a certain

Tankard lid with silversmith's hinge

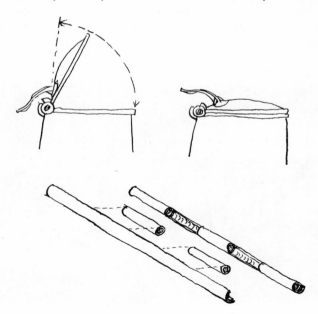

distance the long sections butt against each other and will go no farther. This is a good feature for hot-drink vessels, since the lid when opened might otherwise fall all the way back onto the hand and burn the user.

Hinged bracelets sometimes use two hinges; the hingepin is set in one hinge and removable from the other, so that the second hinge functions as a clasp. The removable hingepin can be attached to the bracelet with a safety-chain should there be a risk of losing the pin otherwise.

By far the most extensive use of hinges is in boxes; the shallow pillbox shown as an exploded drawing at the beginning of this chapter required a spring to keep the lid firmly closed. I have experimented with several types of catches, the most effective being a pin through the front of the box lid, whose lower end is forged and then rolled with a roundnose pliers until it is stiff, with a groove cut into the inside of the front side of the box for it to catch on.

Boxes without hinges can be made with friction-fitted lids; the cast lid of the box shown in the accompanying illustration has a rim of square wire soldered to its underside, the outside of which exactly fits the inner edge of the sides. Such friction-fitting requires a lot of filing, however; moreover, the rim and

Box with cast lid and sides, by J. Coleman

Box on tripod with friction-fitted lid, by D. French

138

sides eventually wear in use so that the fit eventually loosens. I have sometimes added short pins sticking up from the edge of the bottom, with corresponding holes in the lid; this makes it possible for the lid to fit the box only from one position. If you solder an inner rim to the top of the sides of the box, and cut two gaps in it, prongs can be soldered to the top which will hook under the rim except when they are lined up with the gaps.

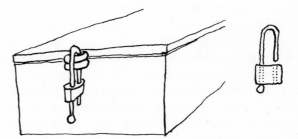

Miniature hasp lock

Sometimes a box lid can be held closed with a miniature hasp and pin: two jump rings, one soldered to the top and the other to the box at the top of one side, can be held together with a pin (an analogy of the hinge clasp mentioned above). An amusing variant of this is a tiny padlock, made by drilling parallel holes in a piece of heavy square stock, inserting a pin (one end of which has been fused to a ball) in one hole and bending the wire around into a hairpin whose free end is just short enough to clear the top of the lock when the hasp is pushed all the way through, but which will slide into the second hole parallel with the first. (Hence the prongs of the hairpin must be the same distance apart as the holes in the body of the lock.) Alternately, a sliding bolt may be made from a piece of square stock and three pieces of wire hammered flat, bent into a C shape to match the bolt, and soldered to the work — two of them to the piece that will hold the bolt and the third on the piece that is to receive it.

Suppose you had made a round box with a cast lid, and wanted to hinge it: If the lid overlaps the bottom by enough distance, it should be possible to hinge the lid by soldering the center section of tubing to the box — either shimming out both sides where the box curves away, or else by sawing a piece out of the top of the side of the box and replacing it with tubing — and soldering the outer two sections to the rim.

A rectangular box can be constructed so that the lid slides off. On three sides of the box, solder a shelf of thin square wire a short distance down from the rim, a little greater than the thickness of the box lid. Solder a strip of flat stock or half-round stock on the upper edge so that it overhangs the inside. The fourth side of the box should be filed down to the height of the tip of the shelf on the other three sides.

Cut a fourth piece of the top molding and solder it to one end of the box lid; the box lid, when filed properly to fit, will slide into the box with the molding piece fitted into the other three-quarters of the molding when the box is completely closed, so that it is not readily apparent how the box opens at all. Moreover, there will be friction of the lid against the box on three sides — enough so that you may want to cut a small notch on the lid, or solder a pin on, so that the user can get a purchase on it to slide it out with a thumbnail.

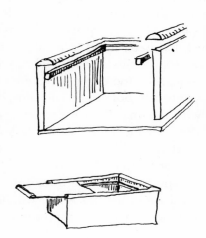

chapter

10

Repairs: Sizing and Special Problems

bezel opening spatula
stone packing (asbestos fiber or "Kool Jool")
jeweler's cement
pearl cement solvent
2 feet easy-flow solder

The chief danger in accepting repair work is your own pride. If a commission is clearly beyond your skill, you will have to steel yourself to say no, both to the crestfallen customer or friend and to your own ego. But the momentary anguish the refusal causes both of you is nothing compared to the ghastly pangs of remorse that come from fouling up a difficult job and having to face the unhappy next-of-kin. Alternately, if you are a depressive type, the tough job sits on the back of your bench for months gathering dust while you "get around to it" (screw your courage to the sticking point). This is the approach which causes ulcers rather than heart failure and is no improvement. I make a rule to do all repairs on the spot or within twenty-four hours, or to decline such jobs when they are impossible (for me), because I decided that this was the only way I could continue to do repair work at all and still keep my peace of mind. I also invariably warn customers that repair work is done at their risk, not mine; mostly, though, I turn down jobs flat that look risky or dubious.

Nevertheless, repair work offers the artisan a lot of opportunity to see how other people's work is put together, and to profit from their example, be it good or bad. Repairs done correctly generate a surprising amount of goodwill, since many shops decline such work altogether. As long as you are cautious, *and humble,* you will not get into trouble on repairs.

The first thing you should do, even before accepting a repair job, is to make sure that the metal is what it is represented to be by the customer. If a piece is stamped *sterling* or *925,* you may be reasonably sure that it *is* sterling and treat it as such. If it is not stamped, but looks like sterling (remember the color differences between sterling, white gold, and steel outlined in Chapter 1), you may probably assume that it is. (But even though sterling, the piece might have been soldered with a low-temperature solder; watch out for this when you heat the work, and have close at hand a couple of sticks of softer solder than you normally use, just in case.)

If the metal looks steely, it might be silver that has been rhodium-plated; if it is stamped sterling you may go ahead with the job but only after agreeing with the customer that the rhodium plating will be burnt off in the process, and if you remove the plating from one earring you should do the other as well. If you are suspicious that the metal is not solid all the way through, but only plating, make an exploratory scratch in some inconspicuous place — inside a ring, for example, or on the back of a pin.

I have said that rhodium plating will be removed; in most cases, this is a good thing as far as I am concerned, but it should be pointed out that the *ideal* repair job is a complete restoration, including whatever finish the object had to begin with. Thus plated work usually will need to be replated, and it is a good idea to know and traffic with the electroplating shop in your local city's jewelers' district (just as it is a good idea to know somebody who can repair silver-plated copper hollowware, Sheffield plate,* and the like. It does you no dishonor to refer work to those who specialize in it if it is not the sort of work that you are able, or wish to be available, to do). By the same token, you should gain some familiarity with tarnishing agents other than liver-of-sulfur; although all tend

---

* A sandwich of thick sheet copper with thin silver sheet bonded to either side; when this is rolled thin the metals retain their proportionate thickness.

toward the same effect, each type tarnishes at different rates and to a slightly different color, and ultimately you will want to know the differences and exploit them to your advantage to do the best job of restoration that you can. As Ross Faneuf put it: "The competent silversmith can repair everything but a deficiency in taste."

The sizing of silver rings without stones is fairly straightforward. If the ring is too small, but was planished in the first place, it can be taken up in size with a planishing hammer; this will work for up to two or three whole sizes, though probably not much further without significantly distorting the original design. If the ring was *not* planished, the most you can stretch it with a rawhide mallet is about a full size, even if you have annealed it. In either case it may be necessary to enlarge the ring by cutting the joint and inserting a short section identical to the band, should the size desired be larger than can be reached by stretching alone.

Sizing *down* a silver ring means cutting a piece out of it; there's no other way, whether the ring wants to go down only a quarter-size or four full sizes. Cut the ring at the existing joint (this also applies if you are sizing it up) and remove enough of the shank that you will be a little under the size you want the ring to be when finished. If you must add a section, form it first to the curvature of the existing ring; this is one job for which a ring stand for soldering is essential, since two joints rather close to each other will have to be soldered, and if you try to solder them while the ring is upside down there will be a tendency for the new section to part company at both joints and fall out. If both joints are soldered while the ring is on the ring stand, the ring will not fall apart even if one joint melts again while you solder the other.

Tom Brown points out that the most serious drawback to having to cut and resolder a ring is that whatever stiffness has been forged or planished into the ring will be lost when the ring is annealed, so that you will have to restore that as well; it's not merely a sizing job. Aside from that, you will

Soldering with a ring stand

Ring packed in asbestos fiber

clearly have to charge more for cutting and resoldering than you do for sizing up with a hammer — unless you wildly overcharge for the latter. Still, it is often the only way to do the job.

Rings with stones are far trickier. There are two ways to cut and resolder a ring with a stone, both with serious drawbacks. Removing the stone from the bezel is time-consuming (hence Tom Brown charges a ten-dollar minimum for such a job), and great care must be taken not to scratch the stone in removing it. Nevertheless, all but the tightest bezels will yield to a thin spatula — an Exacto knife blade that has been dulled with sandpaper works fine here, and is a good deal cheaper than the commercial tool used by watchmakers to pry open watchcases. If you insert the spatula between the bezel and the stone, and work your way around the stone a few times, the stone should be loose enough to pull free.

Another method is quicker but far riskier. You *can* pack the stone in asbestos fiber or heat-sinking foam (sold as a commercial preparation by jewelers' suppliers under the name "Kool-Jool"). This does not always work, though: amethysts sometimes shatter; turquoise almost invariably fries to a charcoal gray; even the bovine agate family is not a sure bet. On the other hand, it takes less than half the time of removing and resetting the stone, and should be considered as a possibility when the joint to be repaired, or the sizing, falls as far away up the shank of a ring as possible. I have used this method successfully dozens of times — in part because I don't use it when it looks too risky.

If a stone is too tight in a bezel, or if the bezel is already damaged, you may have to saw the stone and bezel off and rebuild the whole top of the ring. Occasionally a bezel can be pried loose from the stone it holds, but somebody has thoughtfully cemented the stone in. Ferris' Pearl Cement Solvent, from the jewelers' supplier, will dissolve most cements, including the epoxies; it is indispensable to repairing stones with inlay, which is usually cemented in.

Inlaid stones can be cemented back into place with Hamel-Riglander Quick-Set, Ferris' Pearl Cement, or some other

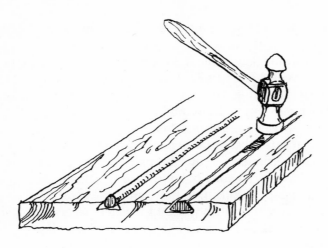

epoxy. If the problem is that a piece of inlay is missing entirely, get another stone the right color, shape unimportant, and crush it to powder. Then mix it up with epoxy into a paste and fill the gap with that.

To inlay silver into wood, make the piece of inlay a little bigger than the space it is to fit and file it down. Sometimes grooves for long inlaid strips of silver are cut with the bottom of the groove wider than the top. A thoroughly annealed piece of round wire (the same thickness as the width of the groove at the surface of the wood) can be laid along the groove and then tapped home with your lightest hammer; the wire will spread down into the sides of the groove. This is easier to do with *fine* silver than with sterling.

If you are brought a ring with enamel-work, use only easy-flow to repair it; the heat required to solder with anything harder will bake the enamel off. Pieces with enamel are often lead-soldered to tie bars, and then the lead solder joint breaks. If you can, get all the lead solder off and solder with easy-flow; but you may have to content yourself with redoing the lead-soldered joint and hoping it lasts longer than it did the first time. I stay away from low-temperature work altogether, sending such jobs elsewhere — life is too short.

Much of the repair work that comes your way will be mechanical failures: hinges break; clasps pull asunder; springy silver in a catch gets overstressed and breaks, or bends out of whack. In the last case, you can usually bend the spring back until the catch works; in the others, you will have to reconstruct. Philip Morton's *Contemporary Jewelry* gives an excellent synopsis of practically every catch on the market, with clear working drawings. Often once you understand the way a catch is supposed to work you can jury-rig a repair without rebuilding the works, bending up a flange here or filing a notch there.

Another common job is converting a piece of jewelry into something else. In this category I would include turning coins into jewelry. A word of caution: it is a federal offense to deface U.S. currency, and that includes soldering to it, boring holes through it, or cutting sections out of it, such as piercing all around the Goddess of Liberty on the old half dollars. Proper coin holders can be purchased from a jewelers' supplier to fit any U.S. coin; if you have an odd-sized coin to set, buy the next larger coin holder and cut a section out of its rim. All of which is perfectly legal, and future generations of numismatists will honor you besides.

Suppose you have a flat-backed piece of silver, other than a coin, that you want to turn into a pin. In many cases you will be able to purchase a one-piece pinstem and catch finding from your jewelers' supplier, in several standard lengths. If you must use separate stems, catches, and sockets, solder the socket first (on the right-hand side), flowing solder onto the back of the piece and then laying the socket on it. After you have pickled the work, line up the pin catch with the socket, either using the pin itself or a long stiff piece of steel wire. If your soldering stylus has a long enough needle, use that; after you have flowed the solder on the back for the catch, lower that into position on the soldering tool, or with a tweezers from the bottom of the piece (hold the catch by the sliding part), so that the open part of the catch faces the top

of the piece (think of your arms carrying firewood). Be very careful not to flow solder between the sliding surfaces of the catch (use yellow ochre beforehand if you are really worried about this). If all goes well, the pin will line up with both socket and catch; if it goes a little out of alignment after you pinch the socket closed on the riveted end, the pin can always be bent a little: hold the socket with flatnosed pliers and bend the pin just as it leaves the socket. Then lop off the extra length of the pin (unless you hit it right on the nose) and file the point again — rounding the tip slightly so it parts the threads of the fabric, rather than ripping the fibers apart, when the pin is worn.

Miscellaneous problems:

(1) *Cracked silver.* About all you can do with the original metal is pickle and flux the crack as clean as you can get it and flow the solder in. If the crack is from the edge of a piece, flow the solder from the inner edge of the crack. The real trouble with cracking is that the metal has been stressed beyond its endurance; you are only patching the weakened area you can see, without remedying an essential structural defect — which, moreover, will probably crop up again further along the lines on dislocation. If at all possible, saw out the weakened and cracked section from the work and replace it with a matching piece of sound metal.

(2) *Cracked stones.* If the stone has cracked or split neatly, you can probably cement it back together. For additional security, cut a cardboard outline of the back of the stone and cement it to that, possibly using a little cement on the bezel as well when you set it. The main drawback to cracked stones is that they are no longer trustworthy as a *structural* element in their setting, however successful a *visual* restoration you may be able to do. Therefore cracked stones must be set in such a way as to bear as little stress as possible, either in setting or in subsequent wear.

(3) *Chipped stones.* Here you are in better shape. If the chip

is down at the edge of a cabochon, you may make a paste of crushed stone and epoxy and restore the surface. (It is a good idea to do this even when the chip is below the bezel, since the wire must still be bent in to fit the contour of the stone and if there is a big dent in one side of the bezel it will be obvious to your colleagues why, and be unbeautiful as well.) Alternately, many stones can be reground with files or a grinding wheel; what a lapidary does with a 10 mm. x 12 mm. stone with a chip in it is regrind it to 9 mm. x 11 mm. If you choose to do this, it will be easier in most cases to affix the stone face up on the end of a *dop stick,* which is a dowel with sealing-wax on one end. This serves as a handle with which you can manipulate it against a grinding wheel or clamp it in a vise for filing.

(4) *Missing stones.* If you have an intact bezel, get a stone to fit it; fitting a stone to an existing bezel means that you have to take the bezel with you to the jewelers' supplier or stone merchant, and try a number of stones from the same lot for fit (and if there are other stones in the setting, for the best color match as well). Otherwise you may find yourself trying to set a stone a little too small for the bezel, resulting in a loose fit; alternately, you may have a stone that is just a little too big which breaks when you try to force it into the bezel. In the case of prong settings, the problem is often that the original setter filed the prongs too thin to begin with. A competent stonesetter can often recut the seat for the stone a little deeper with stonesetters' burrs. As with electroplating and the repairing of Sheffield or other plated work, you will do well to know a reliable diamondsetter in your nearest city, unless you want to make a specialty of such work yourself.

(5) *Irregular stones.* I frequently am asked to make a pendant from a beach stone that the customer picked up on a memorable trip out west, or under circumstances of great sentimental import. I build a wire cage which fits the stone tight on all but one side, with a slack loop of wire there which

I can bend tight and stiff over the stone when I have slipped it into position. If you do this cleverly, you will not need cement to reinforce or immobilize the stone.

(6) *Crystals.* A number of silversmiths have independently invented a setting for tourmaline crystal which, with slight modification, can be used to hold any crystal. The tourmaline is fitted lengthwise between the two ends of a forged U-shaped ring, set slightly into the metal in opposing holes drilled for the purpose. Although a little cement is sometimes used at the point of contact, it is primarily the spring tension of the forged metal that holds the stone in place.

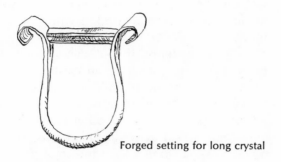

Forged setting for long crystal

chapter
11
Silver Sculpture

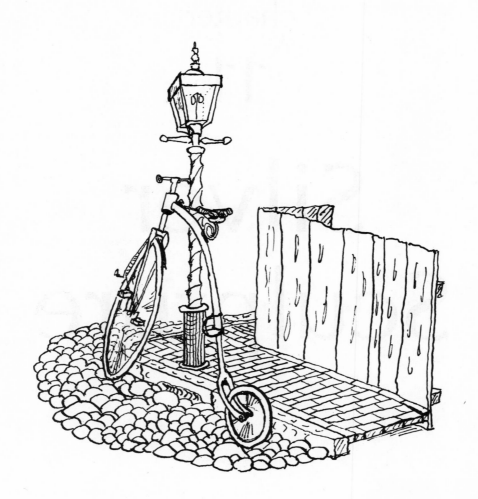

fiberglass brush
protective face mask
watchmaker's hammer
tarnish-removing solution (Tarnex)

"Steam Tractor," by N. Humez

"P-K4 P-K4," by N. Humez

One of the wonders of my childhood — when there was still a wicked old Scollay Square to lure the more adventurous kids in from the suburbs on Saturdays — was Erich Fuchs's exquisite model railroading shop on Tremont Street, still thriving, though Scollay Square fell to the bulldozers years ago. Here I discovered painfully precise models of steam engines in brass, every piston in place, with scrupulous attention to even the most homely details, like the fireman's shovel or the hinges on the firebox door. I came to silversmithing with every intention of doing sculpture on a diminutive scale; indeed, one of the first pieces I did was an arrangement of scrap gleaned from Alan Kueny's scrap heap and purchased from him by weight, the soldering of which I directed (I had not yet learned to solder) but which Doug French and Colin Robertson actually executed. *P-K4 P-K4* was the result — that and a great deal of merriment on the part of Colin and Doug, who wished *they'd* thought of it.

For some time I did sculpture only out of scrap, in part as a way of recycling spoiled work or cutoff ends of wire. The turning point came when I saw an ashtray in the shape of a wheelbarrow in the collection of Philadelphia engraver Michael Flagg. I realized that I too could make wheels that really turned, from scratch, with techniques I was already

155

using in my jewelry. Shortly thereafter I built a bicycle pump and tool kit on a small hillock, with a half-inflated inner tube attached to the pump, to a scale of about two feet to the inch. This was bought by Benjamin Olken, purveyor of fine bicycles to the Humez family over the last thirty-odd years, who also commissioned a bicycle to the same scale.

Although most of my early miniatures were constructed by trial and error, I have found that a rough sketch of the object makes life a lot easier. That way you know what has to fit into what, and the order in which things must be soldered. Moreover, if you do an exploded drawing between the initial sketch and the work, you will have a much clearer notion of your own design, and how far you can depart from it, should you so wish, partway through the construction of the piece. I see this as one advantage of constructed (fabricated) work over cast work: once you have put the model for a casting into the investment, and fired up the burnout kiln, you have shot your bolt.

In making miniatures in silver, it is easy enough to forge the metal on a tiny scale, especially if you have a watch-maker's hammer. The sharp face can be used to crosspeen small pieces of silver much as you use your regular crosspeen for larger ones. Similarly you can dome small pieces of thin sheet on a lead block with the ball end of the chasing or ball peen hammer, or a dapping punch, or a nail whose point you have filed round and polished. You may want to improvise other scaled-down tools from your normal work, depending on what you propose to do in miniature; thus I have used the smooth handle of a broken needle file, set in a vise, as a raising stake. Wooden forming stakes on this scale are, of course, very easily and quickly sawed or filed from scrap hard-wood — it is a good idea to get some fruitwood pieces from an instrumentmaker and carve such stakes from them as the grain tends to be very dense and can be sanded smooth so it will not mark up the work.

Sooner or later, you will want to do miniatures of non-metallic objects. Here the problem will be making the silver

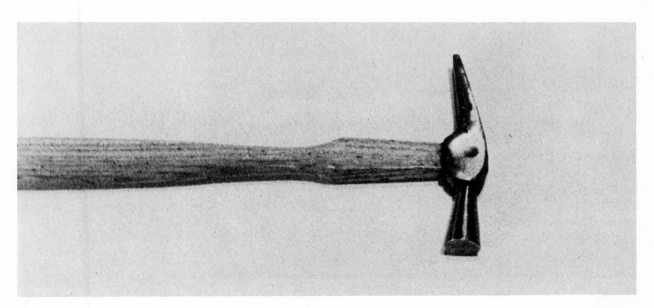

Watchmaker's hammer

"Farm Cart with Forged Tools," by N. Humez

157

Below: Assembling brick sidewalk

look like something else. For wood grain I have found the crosspeen face of the watchmaker's hammer, struck repeatedly and at random along one direction, will simulate the long grain of wood nicely. Nailheads on the wood can be faked with a beading tool. Cobblestones can be made by fusing smallish beads of scrap; curbstone, by rough-planishing heavy square stock to simulate hewn granite; and bricks, by cutting uniform lengths of lighter gauge square stock and bevelling the ends with a file. Tree trunks may be either struck with the watchmaker's hammer or ground with a thin abrasive disc, used edgewise, on the flexible shaft motor, in various patterns according to the bark of the desired tree — I have found elm the easiest, but that comes in part from living in a city where most of the trees on the street are, or were, elms. I have never tried birch, but a few strategically placed shavings with a tiny chisel (make one from a broken filehandle if you need one) might do it.

Tubing is extremely handy, since it can be used as a guide for a spinning axle, or in constructing fitted parts that can be disassembled. For the lamppost I acquired a special kind of

tubing with spiral fluting on the sides, a little like a barber's pole; Boston Findings carries this. For the pedals of bicycles I usually use 18 gauge ID (inside diameter) tubing and an 18 gauge shaft, with 20 gauge pegs soldered on either end for the pedals, which are 20 gauge ID tubing flanked by two short strips of 18 gauge square wire.

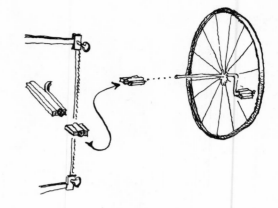

Charcoal casting comes into its own for small details that need to look as if they were cast. The crosspiece on the lamp-post, however, was actually done by fusing the ends of two short pieces of 16 gauge round wire, and then soldering the larger ends to a collar on a post whose top fits the tubing at the bottom of the lantern proper, and whose bottom fits the fluted tubing of the lamppost.

Wheels are a little tricky: the spokes always stretch a little less than the rim when both are heated, so the center of the hub never winds up being precisely where you thought it would be. For this reason there is no point in drilling a hole where the hub is going to be until after the spokes have been soldered to the rim. Usually I solder spokes — a little longer than will be necessary — into a star pattern, and solder the rim separately. Then, when I have formed the rim as round as I can, I take the radius with a pair of dividers, and having struck a small centerpunch mark where the spokes all seem to intersect, use the dividers to mark off the radius on each spoke. Then I cut off the excess spoke ends and solder the spokes to the rim (being careful where the heat is going so as not to melt any spokes while the rim is still heating to solder temperature). Only then do I find the center of the wheel, punch it decisively, and drill it through.

The center of a wheel can be a hole (in which case the wheel will spin freely on a separate axle-pin), a piece of round wire, or a short section of tubing. For both of the latter it is important to make sure that the axle is perpendicular to the wheel — which, like the cube in Chapter 3, requires at least two views. Moreover, the axle will protrude beneath the plane of the soldering pad, so it is well to poke a small hole for it

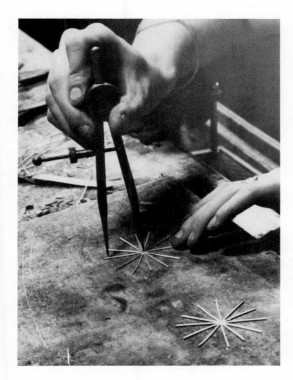

Marking radius of rim on wheel spokes

to rest in. In the case of the front wheel of the pennyfarthing, in which the front axle and pedal crankshaft are one and the same, I soldered the axle on while the wheel rested against a charcoal block. A round-wire axle will allow the wheel to turn freely while held on the sides by a fork with holes drilled at the tips; for best alignment, drill one hole first and then drill the other using the first as a guide. With a tubular axle, the same technique is used, with the advantage that the alignment of the axle with the pin going through it does not depend so critically on the alignment of that pin with the two holes of the fork. This method leaves the pin through the axle free to turn independently of the wheel, although on center with it. Furthermore, the wear will be distributed evenly on the axle pin throughout the inside of the tube, rather than on the holes in the fork.

I have mentioned miniature padlocks earlier under fasteners. Cable chain — straight oval-link chain — can be used for a miniature bicycle chain, and indeed many commercial jewelers' findings can be adapted for use in small sculptures — I once made a soldier's helmet, for example, by fusing the edges of a hollow ¼-inch silver bead away from the hole drilled on one side. The only catch in using standard findings is that other jewelers will readily perceive them as such, and fail to suspend their disbelief enough to view your sculpture as other than a clever amalgamation of findings. And since such pieces will be sold through your colleagues, this may mean that you have to refrain from using findings in sculpture, when they

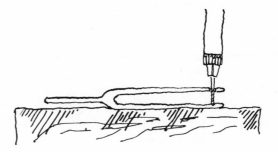

would for all other reasons be appropriate. The same goes for scrap, at least when it remains in a form easily recognizable as spare ends and fused earrings to your fellow silversmiths. One of my sculptures, a shipwreck piece called *St. Elmo's Fire,* was several times declined for display by jewelers who readily took on all the rest of my sculpture: to my colleagues, the ropy sides of the vessel, and the waves underneath, looked uncomfortably like the bangle bracelets made by me from the same stock.

Cleaning and polishing sculptures: Sometimes the shape you have soldered is not one that can easily be gotten into with a buffing wheel. To a certain extent you can get in there with a small bristle wheel on the flexible shaft, but there will still be corners. You *can* brush the corners with a fiberglass brush — if so, use it somewhere where the broken fibers can be safely disposed of, and *always* wear a mask to protect yourself from inhaling any of the vile stuff.

"St. Elmo's Fire," by N. Humez

Another method of curing simple tarnish is to immerse the whole sculpture in a tarnish-removing solution, although this eats a little of the metal away every time you do it. Tumbling the sculpture is probably the best way to polish a piece without any liver-of-sulfur on it; if any parts get bent in the process you can always straighten them later with pliers.

Sometimes you can make polishing easier by designing the piece so it will come apart into several smaller pieces. This is one advantage of having hollow wheel axles, with a pin that can be removed and replaced later: you can clean the wheel separately. In the same way, parts that are riveted together into a swivel joint can be jointed instead by a pin whose point you have sawed in half and bent out; alternately, a 20 gauge rivet can be capped with a short section of 20 gauge ID tubing which you then crimp onto the pin inside with a gentle squeeze of your diagonal cutters. If your sculpture can be taken apart, it will make repairs a lot simpler should the piece be dropped, or some part broken, by a careless owner or shopkeeper.

"Lamppost and Pennyfarthing," by N. Humez, disassembled

chapter
12

Further Business

Tom Brown's workbench

Keep thy shop, said Poor Richard, and thy shop will keep thee. Sooner or later, every silversmith is tempted to go into business: materials are costly (compared, say, to clay), and it is perfectly reasonable that you should sell off a few pieces early on, if only to pay for new tools and supplies. Besides, if word gets around that you do handsome jewelry and some friend turns shopkeeper, you will almost certainly be asked, if not begged, to put some of your work on consignment for sale. And sooner or later a piece does sell, and then you are in business despite yourself.

The positive feedback of somebody admiring your work enough to purchase it is dazzling the first time, and never really wears off; even the thousandth sale gives you a little glow of pride afterwards, as rightly it should. Nevertheless, your *primary* motivating force has to be from within, not only because there will be long days and nights between hurrahs, but also because in order to do truly creative work you must be prepared to buck the tide of popular opinion once in a while, and if you mistake the practice of your craft with a popularity contest you miss the point and your work will soon show it. Still you may wonder, the first few times you sell your work, whether silversmithing might not be a rewarding business to be in, and whether you could scrap your present job for it. After all, the absolute freedom to choose your own hours (providing the work gets done), the joy of working in a creative field and a pliable medium, or even the romance of being the struggling artist, poor but at liberty to do as he or she pleases are all very alluring; and they are all true of making silversmithing your livelihood, up to a point.

But building up a small business is a whole craft unto itself. No matter how much you like making things, selling them when your rent and daily bread depend on it can seem like dreary toil at times; at best it can still seem pretty irrelevant, although being a merchant is not without its own amusements and rewards. Nevertheless, if the practice of your craft is to pay for itself, you will *have* to sell your work somehow, and sell it at a fair price, one that takes into account *all* the actual costs of making it.

No matter how you sell your own work, value it in terms of time (your salary), materials, overhead (a percentage of your shop rent and other general expenses like utilities and paper towels), and profit; the profit, as distinct from your salary, is where the new tools and experimental stuff comes from, although you may choose to allot yourself a budgeted amount for research and development and include it under overhead. The point is that unless you have a shop to work in, fire and metal to work, tools to work the metal with, and some hourly rate for the work, you'll not be able to support the habit, let alone live off the proceeds. Hence you should take all four factors into account when reckoning the selling price of any piece of your work.

I have found that a ledger helps immensely. Mine is divided into four columns for payments and three for sales. The four columns of payments are tools, overhead, materials, and travel; the travel is part of my overhead and you could get by with the first three categories. Sales are divided into out-of-state, in-state for resale, and in-state taxable, primarily for convenience in filling out sales tax returns. (If you live in a state with sales tax, you will need a resale certificate in order to be able to buy materials in that state without paying the

SAMPLE LEDGER
PAGES:
Cash Disbursed . . .

... and Cash Received

CASH DISBURSED 75-3

DATE	ITEMS	TOOLS	CLERICAL	MATERIALS & MANUFACTS	TRAVEL
11 Aug	Balance	4.85	10 78	21 32	4 50
11 Aug	HAGSTOZ			75 81	
13 Aug	Postage to Ocean City N.J.		1 42		
13 Aug	BOSTON FINDINGS, + carfare			51 25	} 50
13 Aug	C.W. Somers	12 78			
14 Aug	Welders' Supply			3 65	
15-18 Aug	Sales trip to N.Y, Phila, L.I. Htfd. total rec'ts				81 33
17 Aug	Keystone Jewelers' Supply, Phila (ziplocks)		19 08		
20 Aug	Boston Findings			8 75	

CASH RECEIVED 75-2

DATE	ITEMS	STATE/SALES TAX	MASS RESALE	RATING MASS. TAXABLE	out-of-state
3 Aug	Ralph Pseudonym: agate pendant	0.75		25 00	
5 Aug	SPURIOUS EMPORIUM Ocean City N.J.				88 25
6 Aug	The Iron Waffle Cambridge MASS		32 50		
7 Aug	TENUBIL MINIATURES Phila. PENNA				175 00
11 Aug	LIMITS, LTD. Northampton MASS		38 00		
11 Aug	The Cellar Hole Dudleytown CT				14 80
13 Aug	E.C. O'goth: a cast pendant+ring			42 50	

state sales tax on them, and in order legally to sell anything at retail in that state. You will also be required to file a state sales tax return listing how much you sold in each of those three categories.) If, on the other hand, all your sales are retail, you need only one column. The important thing is to have an accurate notion of how much money is going for which purposes in order to keep your business afloat. This is the case no matter which of the following roads to market you elect to travel.

Retail. In this system you get 100 percent of the selling price to the customer. On the other hand, you will almost certainly have to keep regular hours in a suitably located retail shop — and by suitably located I mean having sufficient traffic by the shop that you can count on retail sales paying the rent, which is usually priced a little high because everybody else wants to open a shop on a street with good traffic, too, and the landlords know it. If you open on a back street, or out in the country, your rent may be lower but customers may be fewer than can support even a reduced rent. In the city there is the disadvantage that back-street stores are prime targets for burglary and armed robbery, being relatively low-risk jobs for the felon since police protection and sophisticated protective hardware are generally concentrated at major areas of foot traffic. Out in the country, on the other hand, you may get considerable seasonal traffic from vacationers, one very good reason why many silversmiths in New England first set up shop on Cape Cod, at least before the rents really soared down there. The trick seems to be to figure out where the beautiful people or whatever are all going to summer two years from now, and then get in there this year and sign a five-year lease. I do not recommend this: for one thing it leaves you no time to do silver between Memorial Day and Labor Day.

Wholesale. Here you sell at 50 percent (or slightly less) of the retail price; for their 100 percent markup the retailers save you the considerable bother of keeping those hours, paying

A back-street silversmith's shop

those rents, dealing with all those people, and taking the risk on whether the store will make it or have to fold. This method of selling is often used to augment the income of retail stores in their early years, but it can be an adequate source of income by itself, as my own experience will testify. Wholesaling requires much less time spent on actual selling, since the orders tend to be larger. It is easy for one silversmith to supply a dozen shops with, say, two dozen pairs of earrings, a dozen rings, and six bangle bracelets per month, and live comfortably on the proceeds: easy providing you are willing to make three dozen of the same thing every month or two, which not everybody is. Nonetheless, wholesaling *will* keep the wolf from the door, and leave you one week free in four for research and development; nearly every silversmith has weathered a storm by judicious wholesaling.

A disadvantage to wholesaling is that you wind up making a lot of the same thing, instead of a new thing every time. This alone is a good reason for not wanting to stay a wholesaler forever; many silversmiths also abandon wholesaling when their retail trade gets brisk.

Jobbers. These merchants buy in huge lots from manufacturers or production houses, and sell at wholesale, or slightly under. The idea is that you, the manufacturer, can give anybody a break on quantity in exchange for having to spend as little sales time as possible. Occasionally wholesalers with over a dozen people working for them will find it preferable to keep a crew working and sell off their work through a jobber at less than wholesale. The real solution is never to let your business become so unwieldy that you are forced to do this. The simplest way is to wholesale alone, or perhaps with a partner at most, and to limit production, or there will be no time left for research and development, let alone Great Art. This means saying no to more work than you can take on, and hence saying no to your wallet occasionally. I learned this by soldering six dozen triple circle earrings for a fellow from Quincy, to whom I am eternally indebted for the lesson not to do it again.

Consignment. This is the most profitable form of wholesaling, since the retailer with whom you consign your work pays you only after the piece has sold, and in return gives you typically a larger cut of the cake, two thirds rather than one half. All shows of my sculpture have been on this basis, as galleries usually are run under a consignment agreement also. It is frequently the only way to get your jewelry or other work shown in stores with limited capital, and is almost always readily open to the silversmith just starting out in business. It ties up stock, though; usually this is less burdensome when you are an established wholesaler or retailer rather than right at the beginning of your career. Nevertheless, consignment is the only way of selling a really expensive piece if you do not have a retail shop of your own.

Crafts demonstrations. Sometimes schools or other non-profit organizations will approach you to come out and demonstrate silversmithing for a day. Usually this is an arrangement where you are not paid to move your shop out and back, but you are allowed or encouraged to sell, with the house taking one fifth to one third of your sales. I accept as many such demonstration engagements as I can: they are great fun, and usually sales are good. If you are approached to do a demonstration at which sales will not be allowed, charge your regular working rate for the hours of the demonstration plus your expenses in getting your shop out and back. An honest client will pay these expenses willingly, or at least acknowledge their fairness.

Flea markets, etc. Under the usual arrangement you pay the house a flat fee for a table (or space for it), and perhaps a percentage as well. I will occasionally do one of these, but only if there are not already four or five silversmiths selling their wares. Otherwise the house is pitting you against your colleagues. If you elect to rent space at one of the great flea markets (Faneuil Hall in Boston or the Philadelphia Flea Market, for example), check it out as a customer first.

Advertising and catalogues. If you have a flourishing wholesale trade you may never need to advertise, but you will find

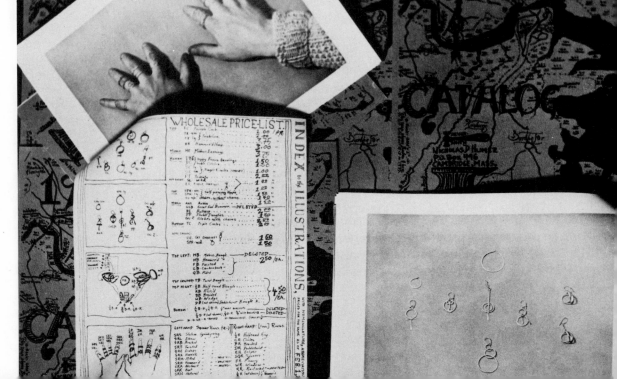

it handy to have a catalogue of your regular stock in trade, not only for mailing to new contacts but also to give your existing clients so they will know what to call things when they reorder them. In addition, you may want to place an advertisement in a periodical to sell a particularly extravagant piece or to encourage people to write for your catalogue and order from it. Catalogues should contain pictures, names and prices of each item; line-drawings will do but photographs are better.

Photographing silver is a little tricky since the highlights tend to be very "hot" when you light the work directly; on the other hand, totally diffused light leaves the silver looking like dull pewter. The best combination seems to be diffused light plus a small spot or "hair-light"; shoot the silver on a white, nonreflective background and shield the sides from direct light by a curving wall of the same material — heavy construction paper, poster board, or even the back side of shelf-lining paper from the local five and dime.

Shop design. In laying out your workshop, it helps to separate your operation into several mutually exclusive parts: soldering should go in one corner, buffing in another, drawing in a third, and display in a fourth, with other operations in other areas as you see fit. You could do all your bookkeeping at a desk in the display area, or at your drawingboard, for example. Or your buffing wheel and stake-holder could be attached at opposite ends of the same workbench. Drawings of three shop plans are shown here. Note that in the two retail shops the area open to the customer is set off from the manufacturing and bookkeeping zone. Note too that the workbench is placed in such a position that its occupant can watch all the area open to the public while he or she works.

No shop is complete without a good technical library. Minimum requirements (besides the present book, of course):
Bovin, Murray. *Jewelry Making.* Forest Hills, N.Y.: Bovin Publishing, 1967, revised 1971. A concise manual and reference

Lighting arrangement to photograph silver

Floor plans for three retail silversmith's shops.

Top: Fire and Metal, Burlington, Vt.;
center: Designers 3, Cambridge, Mass. (in 1968);
bottom: Silver Smithed, Rockport, Mass.

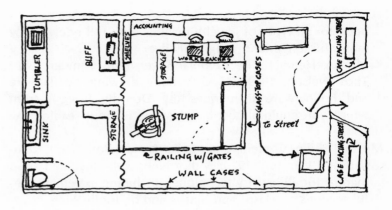

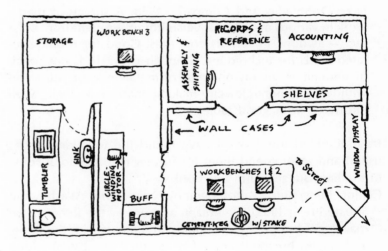

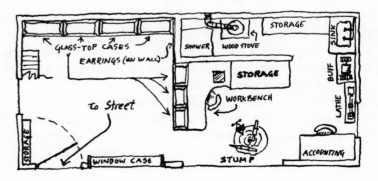

book for all types of jewelry making, with full equivalency tables for length and weight of silver.

Kauffman, Henry J. *The Colonial Silversmith*. Camden, N.J.: Thos. Nelson, 1969. Good working drawings of flatware and hollowware techniques (by Dorothy Briggs), from which you could almost learn raising without reading the text.

Morton, Philip. *Contemporary Jewelry*. New York: Holt, Rinehart and Winston, 1970. A thorough, well-illustrated shop manual for all jewelry techniques, including extremely useful sections on clasps and hinges and on toolmaking.

Untracht, Oppi. *Metal Techniques for Craftsmen*. Garden City, N.Y.: Doubleday and Company, 1968. A survey of metalwork in various media — silversmithing, wrought iron, brass etc. — as done in various countries. Good for robbing related fields for techniques, although Untracht is not specific enough about any one type of metalwork for you to do without a general jewelry-making manual as well. Well illustrated with good tables.

In addition to the above I have found the following books useful and recommend them for further reading along some of the lines suggested in this book:

Cellini, Benvenuto. *Autobiography*. New York: Washington Square Press, 1963. The brazen account by the Renaissance master goldsmith of his triumphs, arguments with the Pope, and narrow escape from violent death. A great yarn with a lot of information about the Renaissance Italian workshop, especially casting techniques.

Goffman, Erving. *Relations in Public*. New York: Harper/Colophon, 1972. Chapters entitled "The Territories of the Self" and "Normal Appearances" are particularly relevant to retail shop design and security.

Henderson, James. *Silver Collecting for Amateurs*. London: Frederick Muller, 1965. A quick, readable survey of English silversmithing from 1600 to 1900, with a discussion of the

British hallmarking system and chronological hallmark tables.

Kauffman, Henry J. *American Axes*. Brattleboro, Vt.: Stephen Greene Press, 1972. Explains a lot about hot-forging iron, lucidly illustrated by Dorothy Briggs.

Klee, Paul. *Pedagogical Sketchbook* (1925). Trans. Sybil Moholy-Nagy. New York: Frederick Praeger, 1953. A real eye-opener on design, one of fourteen Bauhaus books issued under the auspices of Walter Gropius in the 1920s. Very astute section on asymmetric design and balance.

Pirsig, Robert M. *Zen and the Art of Motorcycle Maintenance*. New York: Bantam, 1974. An invigorating autobiographical ramble, with a sound defense of the concept of *quality* in life and art. A seminar in thinking clearly.

Pye, David. *The Nature and Art of Workmanship*. New York: Van Nostrand and Reinhold, 1968. Debunks some popular notions about handwork and proposes a new classification of workmanship into that of *risk* opposed to that of *certainty*.

Ruskin, John. "The Nature of Gothic," Ch. 6 of *The Stones of Venice*, vol. II (1853). Reprinted in Matthew Hodgart, ed., *Selected Prose of Ruskin*. New York: Signet (New American Library), 1972. The classic Victorian humanist plea for meaningful work, and against the dehumanization of nineteenth-century factory life. Ruskin insists that quality of life on a society-wide scale is reflected in the quality of that society's art.

Here are sources of metal and tools, mostly in the Northeast. This is a partial and idiosyncratic list, but it should get you started, and you will turn up other sources as you need them. For a full selection of each company's offerings, write to each for a catalogue.

Allcraft, 215 Park Ave., Hicksville, N.Y. 11401. (Tools)

A.R.E., Box 155, Plainfield, Vermont 05667. (Metal)

Boston Findings and Jewelers' Supply, 373 Washington St., Rm. 501, Boston, Mass. 02108. (General)

Paul H. Gesswein and Co., 235 Park Avenue South, New York, N.Y. 10003. (Tools)

T. B. Hagstoz and Son, 709 Sansom St., Philadelphia, Pa. 19106. (General)

Rio Grande Jewelers' Supply, 6901 Washington N.E., Albuquerque, N.M. 87109. (Metal)

Keystone Jewelers' Supply, 713 Sansom St., Philadelphia, Pa. 19106 (Ziplok bags)

C. W. Somers, 387 Washington St., Rm. 509, Boston, Mass. 02108. (General)

Terra-Cotta, 765 Massachusetts Ave., Cambridge, Mass. 02139. (General)

Myron Toback, 23 W. 47th St., New York, N.Y. 10036. (General)

Woodstock Craft Tools, Inc., 21 Tinker St., Woodstock, N.Y. 12498. (General, including lapidary supplies)

"Faneuf's Grindstone," by N. Humez